THRIVE:

Igniting Your Inner Fire for a Fulfilled Life

BY LANE HAWKINS

All emphasis in the text (*italics*) is the authors adding.

Cover Photo taken by **Andrew Mandemaker - 2006**
https://en.m.wikipedia.org/wiki File:Sunset_with_coconut_palm_tree,_Fiji.jpg

THRIVE:Thrive: Igniting Your Fire for a Fulfilled Life
ISBN 978-0-9667955-1-6

Joint-Heir Publishing

Printed in the United States of America

Table of Content

Acknowledgments   1

Introduction   6

Are you Surviving or Thriving?   8

The Survivalist Mindset   14

Transitioning from Surviving to Thriving   28

What is the Daniel Fast?   40

Why make Declarations?   46

1. We were created to thrive   50

2. The Principle of Release   62

3. The Principle of Harvest   79

4. The Principle of Potential   93

5. The Principle of Endurance   110

6. The Principle of Overcoming Crisis   125

Final thoughts   136

About the Author   137

ACKNOWLEDGMENTS

I want to express my gratitude to the individuals and groups who have played a crucial role in laying the foundation for this work to come to fruition in my life.

I want to express my deep appreciation and affection for my wonderful wife, Toyea. Our journey together has been nothing short of amazing, starting from high school and continuing through the challenges and triumphs of life. I feel truly fortunate to have you as my partner, and I treasure every moment we share.

To Kayla, Kahlia, Toyea Jr., and Loreigna, my amazing and talented children, you are all incredibly unique and cherished by me. My heart is filled with love and gratitude for each one of you.

To my Parents:
My mom Creasie, I cannot thank you enough for your steadfast love and care. Your prayers for me have not gone unanswered, and I am forever grateful for your unwavering support. My love for you runs deep and cannot be put into words.

To Daniel, I wanted to express how much I miss you and extend my gratitude for getting me started. I wish we had more time together.

To Wilbert, I often find myself overwhelmed with thoughts of you, and it's clear how much your absence affects me. Thank you for laying the foundation.

To Joanne, I am grateful for your role in my growth from an uncertain teenager to who I am today. Your unwavering love and support have been unmistakable. I cherish you deeply.

To James and Mel, your continual encouragement has been fantastic, and your love for me has been undeniable. Thank you for all of your support.

Thrive: Igniting Your Fire for a Fulfilled Life

To Mary (Momma) and Sam (Daddy), every time I think of you, Mom, it brings tears to my eyes because I miss you so much. No words can truly convey my appreciation for both of you; please know that I am forever thankful to both of you.   You two saved my life.

To my siblings
Erica (Pinky) and Greg, Eric (Knuckle) and Machell; Elicia (Pumpkin); Kent and CJ; Kirk and Denise; Danny and Marion

To my Neighborhood Family
I can't mention all of your names, but know that I love you!

My Horsemen brothers:
Kent, Willie, Michael, and Eric

My Coaching Fraternity
Bert, Marlon, Bobby, Mark, Dave (Big Super), Dominguez, Rob, Kirby, Kameron, Frank, Teron, and Gene.

I want to express my gratitude to Rowena and Toni for their attentiveness and keen observation skills.

"My mission in life is not merely to survive, but to THRIVE; and to do so with some passion, some compassion, some humor, and some style."   **– Maya Angelou**

John 10:10 The thief comes only in order to steal and kill and destroy. I came that they may have and enjoy life, and have it in abundance [to the full, till it overflows]. - AMP

INTRODUCTION

Welcome to THRIVE: Igniting your Inner Fire for a fulfilled life, a 40-day devotional that will help you tap into your inner fire and live a truly fulfilling life.

Have you ever questioned whether there is more to life than what you are currently experiencing? Or perhaps you have lost the passion that fuels you, leaving you feeling drained and burdened by everything.

Then this unique devotional, incorporating a 40-Day Daniel fast to enhance your spiritual progress, is for you.

With this devotional, you will embark on a journey of self-discovery, growth, and transformation as you learn how to reignite your passion for life, fulfill your God-given purpose, and walk into your ability to thrive.

You're about to explore the biblical principles and practical strategies to overcome the obstacles holding you back and create a life filled with joy, purpose, and fulfillment. Each day, you will be guided through a scripture reading, reflection, prayer, and practical application to help you tap into your inner fire and thrive in every aspect of your life.

Through this devotional, you will learn several principles to help you ignite your inner fire and live a fulfilling life.

You will discover how to:

- release what is holding you back,
- reap a bountiful harvest,
- recognize your potential,
- develop endurance, and
- overcome crises

40 Days of Transformation

You will be guided to self-discovery, spiritual growth, and transformation that can enable you to live a life that honors God and brings you joy and purpose.

Are you ready to ignite your inner fire and live a life of fulfillment? Let's begin this 40-day journey together and see what God has in store for you.

ARE YOU SURVIVING OR THRIVING?

Success and abundance are our natural state.   - **Dr. James B. Richards**

God created us to thrive and not survive - to live a life of purpose, joy, and fulfillment.

When we closely examine Scripture, we can see this. Let's go back to Genesis 2:16.

> **Genesis 2:16** And the Lord God commanded the man, saying, "Of every tree of the garden you may freely eat;

Do you understand the significance of this verse? It proclaims that we can thrive. The deliberate use of "every" and "freely" emphasizes God's plan for us to flourish.

But yet, many of us don't; thus, we find ourselves limping through life, surviving.

Many of us don't truly thrive because we never decide to.

What's the difference between thriving and surviving? Surviving is getting by, maintaining, or existing with enough to sustain ourselves. But thriving refers to experiencing an abundant and fulfilling life.

> **John 10:10** ... I have come that you might have life (Zoe) and have it more abundantly.

Let me give you an example of the difference between surviving and thriving. Do you remember the story of Ruth? (Read Ruth 2.) When Ruth returned to Bethlehem, she had to glean in the field of Boaz. She had to rely on leftovers on the ground and in the corners of the field. This is survival: existing with enough. Just enough to live on. Just enough to make it to the next day.

Survival is not natural, it is learned!

But Ruth's destiny was not to survive; it was to thrive. She married Boaz and transitioned from gathering leftovers to owning the field. This is the difference between surviving and thriving. If survival is getting by, then thriving is about experiencing abundant life.

Surviving isn't only about a lack of possessions. A limiting belief system also prevents us from living a full life. Consider the Children of Israel, who spent forty years wandering in the wilderness after their captivity in Egypt. Although they walked with God and received His provisions and care, their experience was surviving rather than thriving. Let's go further.

In nature, wild animals have an innate drive called "survival instinct." It's this instinct that enables them to live and avoid death. Losing this instinct leads to their demise.

Surviving can be a never-ending cycle, like riding a merry-go-round that offers no real view and no way off. I've experienced moments when I've felt stuck. It wasn't because of a particular sin but rather a lack of progress. It felt like I was wandering in the wilderness with no direction. I was going through all the motions, knowing all the right words and actions but missing the true connection with God. Life was bland and dull. I now realize I was surviving rather than thriving.

Recently, I had a personal revelation that there was so much more. I wanted more of Him in my life. So, I turned to the Word for guidance and found myself in Jeremiah 17. It was here that I came to understand my condition of survival mode.

Jeremiah 17:5 Thus says the Lord, "Cursed is the man who trusts in man And makes flesh his strength, Whose heart departs from the Lord. **6** For he shall be like a shrub in the desert, And shall not see when good comes But shall inhabit the parched places in the wilderness, In a salt land which is not inhabited".

Thrive: Igniting Your Fire for a Fulfilled Life

What a vivid picture of surviving and being in a constant state of stress and uncertainty. In such situations, we rely on our strength, resources, and ideals rather than turning to God for guidance. We focus on immediate needs and challenges and struggle to see beyond the difficulties of the present moment. And we don't produce any fruit in our lives. All these go against God's design, and it was here that I knew I needed to explore other options beyond surviving.

This was my "burning bush" moment. Like Moses, I turned aside to hear the question, "Are you thriving or surviving?" Have you ever heard this question? It's simple yet profound and can impact how we approach our lives. Take a moment to reflect on this question and your answer.

As believers, we can find ourselves in a spiritual desert, feeling barren and unfruitful. In these moments, our language reflects our emptiness. We say things like "Thank God it's Friday" or "Only a few more minutes left." These words serve as a revelation of the state of our hearts. They indicate that we're in survival mode, looking for the nearest exit from the "Merry-Go-Round" of life. Survival holds us in a vicious cycle. It's a lifetime merry-go-round without a view. We could better understand our current situation if we were mindful of our language.

> Survival is a vicious cycle. It's a lifetime merry-go-round, without the view.

One of the biggest hurdles we face is the tranquilizing effects of survival mode. It keeps us trudging along without experiencing true satisfaction. So, we find ourselves stuck in a monotonous routine, a rut if you will, around and around we go, with no hope of escaping. We are surviving.

Picture the theme music of the Twilight Zone playing. Here's my version:

There is a fifth dimension beyond that which is known to man. It is a dimension as vast as space and as timeless as infinity. It is the middle ground between light and shadow, between science and superstition, and between the pit of man's fears and the summit of his knowledge. This is the dimension of no imagination, no life, and no hope. It is an area which is called the Survival Zone.

Yet, God did not create us to survive but to thrive! Let's declare this truth together: "God created me to thrive!" Thriving refers to having a dynamic and flourishing relationship with God. Thriving means living a life of purpose, joy, and fulfillment. It's utilizing the gifts and talents that God has given us to positively impact the world around us.

Let's revisit Jeremiah 17:7-8

> **Jeremiah 17:7** - "Blessed is the man who trusts in the Lord, And whose hope is the Lord. **8** For he shall be like a tree planted by the waters, Which spreads out its roots by the river And will not fear when heat comes; But its leaf will be green, And will not be anxious in the year of drought, Nor will cease from yielding fruit.

The key to thriving is placing our trust in the Lord. When this happens, we find the following :

- A thriving person is like a tree planted by the waters, with deep roots stretching out.
- A thriving person remains green and fruitful and does not fear or become anxious.
- A thriving person experiences peace and stability through difficult circumstances.
- A thriving person grows and bears fruit.

Isn't this powerful? We have a beautiful experience and a full and prosperous life through our trust in God. This is what it means to thrive. And for most of my life, I wasn't experiencing this. Life was happening to me, and I was merely a passive observer, tossed around by the waves of circumstance. In short, I was surviving.

So, let me ask you, "Are you tired of surviving? Are you ready to thrive?" If you are ready, remember that thriving isn't automatic. If you want to thrive, you must decide you are no longer willing to merely survive. I know this sounds simple, but it's the truth. You can begin thriving today by choosing to follow the principles of God, which leads us to thrive.

THE SURVIVALIST MINDSET

You don't have to control your thoughts; you just have to stop letting them control you. - **Dan Millman**

Have you ever watched any of those Survivor TV shows? *Alone, The Ultimate Survivor, Life below Zero*, and my favorite, *Naked and Afraid.*

The common theme in many of these shows is that the participants think differently. Their whole way of processing is based on what I must do to survive the day. Maybe today, I forage for food; tomorrow, I work on the shelter, and the next day I'll do this or that. It's really about making it through the day.

If I am ever stranded on some barren tropical island, I hope I remember everything from these shows.

But for the believer, how do we obtain this survivalist mindset?

Let's look at Gideon, whose life exemplified someone with a survival mindset; even though he became a leader and warrior, who defeated the Midianites under God's power, he did not start that way. He was initially fearful and lacked confidence.

> **Judges 6.11** Now the Angel of the Lord came and sat under the terebinth tree which was in Ophrah, which belonged to Joash the Abiezrite, while his son Gideon threshed wheat in the winepress, in order to hide it from the Midianites. **12** And the Angel of the Lord appeared to him, and said to him, "The Lord is with you, you mighty man of valor!" **13** Gideon said to Him, "O my lord, if the Lord is with us, why then has all this happened to us? And where are all His miracles which our fathers told us about, saying, 'Did not the Lord bring us up from Egypt?' But now the Lord has forsaken us and delivered us into the hands of the Midianites." **14** Then the Lord turned to him and

said, "Go in this might of yours, and you shall save Israel from the hand of the Midianites. Have I not sent you?" **15** So he said to Him, "O my Lord, how can I save Israel? Indeed my clan is the weakest in Manasseh, and I am the least in my father's house." **16** And the Lord said to him, "Surely I will be with you, and you shall defeat the Midianites as one man."

This is an excellent example of what it means to have a survivor mindset. Just look at the picture of Gideon:

The first thing about the Survivalist Mindset is that it forces you into hiding.

> **11** Now the Angel of the Lord came and sat under the terebinth tree which was in Ophrah, which belonged to Joash the Abiezrite, while his son Gideon threshed wheat in the winepress, in order to hide it from the Midianites.

Gideon is hiding-both physically and metaphorically. His actions are driven by fear, which further compounds his struggles. His fear paralyzes him and prevents him from stepping out of his survival zone and embracing new possibilities - his ability to thrive.

When we have a survival mindset, we operate in a state of fear and without a clear vision. And like Gideon, the absence of a compelling vision will keep us trapped in a cycle of confusion and uncertainty, where we lack a sense of direction and purpose.

Additionally, our location and actions do not align with our true selves. It's as if we wander aimlessly, engaging in activities that do not contribute to our personal growth or fulfillment. Despite exerting a lot of effort, we fail to achieve meaningful results. This mismatch between our location, actions, and desires further exacerbates our confusion and frustration.

Hiding also represents a noticeable absence of a willingness to fight in our lives, lacking the resilience and determination to confront the challenges and obstacles that come our way. This unwillingness to engage in the battle for our dreams and aspirations will keep us stagnant and hinders our progress. We'll retreat and avoid conflict or adversity instead of standing up and embracing the struggle.

The second thing about the Survivalist Mindset is your language.

As he is hiding, the Angel of the Lord called him, "You mighty man of valor," but Gideon's language and mindset revealed that he is in survival mode. Look at his reply in verse 13:

> **13** Gideon said to Him, "O my lord, if the Lord is with us, why then has all this happened to us? And where are all His miracles which our fathers told us about, saying, 'Did not the Lord bring us up from Egypt?' But now the Lord has forsaken us and delivered us into the hands of the Midianites."

His language is littered with hopelessness and blame.

When the Angel of the Lord appears to Gideon, calling him to rise and lead his people, Gideon's reply in verse 13 highlights his negative perspective. He questions the presence of God and the absence of miracles, expressing his doubts and frustrations. Gideon's words imply that he perceives himself and his people as forsaken and delivered into the hands of their enemies the Midianites.

Gideon reinforces his sense of hopelessness and powerlessness by voicing his doubts and focusing on the perceived absence of divine intervention. His language becomes a self-fulfilling prophecy, supporting his negative beliefs and inhibiting his ability to recognize his true potential as a leader and warrior.

Gideon's language is a powerful reminder of how our words can impact our mindset and actions. But according to scripture, our words result from what's filled in our hearts. When we allow hopelessness and doubt to dominate our language, we limit our ability to rise above challenges and tap into our inherent strength.

Gideon's example teaches us the importance of speaking words of faith, resilience, and empowerment, even in the face of adversity.

The third thing about the Survivalist Mindset is that it only sees what it doesn't have.

Gideon didn't have any peace. He didn't have any faith in God's ability to deliver them.

All he could focus on was hiding from the Midianites so they wouldn't come to take his food. He was all about preservation. He was trying to out-smart the problem instead of trusting in God's power.

Let's look at Matthew 16:5-8

> **Matthew 16: 5** And when his disciples were come to the other side, they had forgotten to take bread. **6** Then Jesus said unto them, Take heed and beware of the leaven of the Pharisees and of the Sadducees. **7** And they reasoned among themselves, saying, It is because we have taken no bread. **8** Which when Jesus perceived, he said unto them, O ye of little faith, why reason ye among yourselves, because ye have brought no bread? **9** Do ye not yet understand, neither remember the five loaves of the five thousand, and how many baskets ye took up?

In the previous chapter, Jesus performs one of His greatest miracles, feeding the multitude with two fish and five loaves of bread. Now as we come to verse 8, he notices the disciples talking among themselves about what they don't have. They didn't have any bread. But Jesus' comment in verse 8 is extremely powerful because when we have a survivalist mindset, it tends to be the launching pad for our actions and decisions. He states:

> **8** Which when Jesus perceived, he said unto them, O ye of little faith, why reason ye among yourselves, because ye have brought no bread?

In other words, "Why are you starting at what you don't have?" Then verse 9 comes with the hammer: Don't you remember... the five loaves used to feed the five thousand? But, when you've been surviving, this seems normal: to lock in and focus on what you don't have.

The survivalist mindset, characterized by its focus on immediate needs and resources, further reinforces the tendency to see only what is currently available. This mindset arises from a sense of urgency and the need to meet basic survival requirements. There must be more room for long-term vision or strategic planning in such a mindset.

When operating from a survivalist mindset, it's easy to prioritize short-term necessities, such as food, shelter, and safety. This narrow focus often leads to tunnel vision solely concentrating on immediate concerns. As a result, the ability to perceive and pursue broader possibilities and opportunities becomes restricted.

Gideon's survivalist mindset contributes to his limited vision. The survivalist mindset prevents him from considering alternative strategies, seeking alliances, or envisioning a future beyond the present circumstances. He becomes consumed with the immediate challenges the Midianites pose to the point where he fails to recognize his potential and the broader possibilities for his people.

However, it is crucial to recognize that a survivalist mindset is limiting. While it serves a purpose in times of immediate crisis, it restricts growth and hinders the development of a broader vision. It perpetuates a cycle of constantly focusing on what is at hand without allowing for exploring new opportunities or pursuing long-term goals.

We must intentionally shift our perspective to overcome the constraints of a survivalist mindset. This involves recognizing that while immediate needs are essential, there is value in considering long-term goals, aspirations, and possibilities. By expanding our focus beyond immediate survival, we can tap into our creativity, resourcefulness, and resilience to chart a path towards growth and fulfillment.

Instead of appreciating the resources and abilities at Gideon's disposal, he fixates on his perceived deficiencies. This mindset creates a negative feedback loop, reinforcing feelings of dissatisfaction and hindering personal growth. Thus keeping us locked into this vicious cycle of survival.

This way you learned to survive, may not be the way you want to live.

His complaints highlight his tendency to attribute fault to God. He perceives his struggles and hardships as evidence of divine abandonment. This belief distances him from a sense of personal agency, as he relinquishes responsibility for his own choices and actions.

However, it is crucial to recognize the limitations of such a perspective. Blaming God for our circumstances is an avoidance tactic that shields us from personal growth and development. It absolves us of the responsibility to take control of our lives and make necessary changes.

By focusing on what he doesn't have and placing blame on God, he fails to see the power within himself to effect change. Instead of complaining, he can shift his perspective and embrace gratitude. Gratitude cultivates a mindset of abundance, allowing us to recognize the blessings and opportunities surrounding us. It shifts our focus from what is lacking to what we have, fostering a sense of contentment and empowerment.

The fourth thing about the Survivalist Mindset is that it causes us to function as victims and not victors.

Victim. That's what a lot of people in our world feel like. And many of them have been victims of neglect, abuse, gossip, a broken family, tragedy, or rejection. The wounds are real.

Thrive: Igniting Your Fire for a Fulfilled Life

Navigating life can be challenging as we encounter numerous obstacles and unexpected twists and turns. While it's important to acknowledge the reality of these struggles and pains, but we must not allow them to define our character or dictate our responses. As believers, it's crucial to conduct ourselves in a manner that reflects our devotion to Jesus Christ and to always remember that our identity is rooted in the salvation He has bestowed upon us.

Let's look at verse 13 again:

> **13** Gideon said to Him, "O my lord, if the Lord is with us, why then has all this happened to us? And where are all His miracles which our fathers told us about, saying, 'Did not the Lord bring us up from Egypt?' But now the Lord has forsaken us and delivered us into the hands of the Midianites."

Gideon blames God for his predicament. It's not my fault. It's because of this or that!

One day, my wife and I were driving to church. As we were crossing the Bay Bridge, another driver did something to cause my wife to blurt out: "Shoot, you gonna make me mad!" I glanced over to her, as I was driving, and I made this statement: " You are too beautiful, smart, and intelligent to give away that much power in your life by allowing someone else to make you mad."

This is what a survivalist mindset causes us to do - play the victim.

The victim believes the whole world is against them; the victor believes the whole world needs them.

The victim sees a challenge as an obstacle; the victor sees the obstacle as an opportunity.

A victim focuses on outward pressures, while a victor focuses on inward reality.

A victim only sees problems; a victor sees solutions.

The victim gives up quickly if they don't succeed; the victor doesn't quit until they succeed.

The victim underachieves; the victor overachieves.

The victim feels like they can't succeed, while the victor feels like they must succeed.

Let's look at Gideon's statement in verse 15:

> **15** So he said to Him, "O my Lord, how can I save Israel? Indeed my clan is the weakest in Manasseh, and I am the least in my father's house."

I'm too small to do anything. I don't have enough education. I'm the wrong color. And the list could go on. His statement has an essence of truth: His clan is the smallest, and he is the least in his father's house, but it is not the truth of who he was. You see, that's part of the victim mentality. Pervert the truth so you can remain a victim!

Through the power of Christ, He has made us free and established us as conquerors.

The choice is yours to determine what defines you; your pain or your possibilities, your events or your attitude, your past or your future, your wounds or the wounds of Jesus when He sacrificed Himself for you.

Make the choice today to let go of being a victim and rise to your true position as a Victor!

The fifth thing about the survivalist mindset is that it fails to achieve its potential.

Let's look at verses 14-15;

14 Then the Lord turned to him and said, "Go in this might of yours, and you shall save Israel from the hand of the Midianites. Have I not sent you?" **15** So he said to Him, "O my Lord, how can I save Israel? Indeed my clan is the weakest in Manasseh, and I am the least in my father's house."

This aspect will cause us to only offer excuses for not being productive or living below the standards of life.

This occurs when individuals resist accepting the truth of who they are and what they are capable of. It exemplifies this struggle of Gideon's questioning of God's presence, power, and qualifications.

Gideon finds it challenging to receive and embrace the truth of his identity in the grip of a survivalist mindset. Despite being addressed as a "mighty man of valor" by the Angel of the Lord, he questions whether God is truly with them. This doubt reflects his lack of faith in God's guidance and intervention.

Moreover, he undermines his potential by questioning God's power. He fails to recognize the limitless possibilities and resources available through a connection with God. This skepticism hampers his ability to tap into a higher source of strength, wisdom, and guidance that could empower him to achieve extraordinary feats.

Finally, he makes excuses based on his perceived limitations within his family and clan. By clinging to these excuses, he prevents himself from stepping into his true identity as a leader and warrior. He allows his background and status to overshadow his true potential.

This resistance to the truth and reliance on excuses forms a self-imposed barrier that inhibits personal growth and hinders realizing one's potential. Gideon's inability to fully accept and embrace his identity as a chosen instrument of God's purpose limits his ability to rise above his circumstances and fulfill his true calling.

To overcome this limitation, it is essential to confront and dismantle the barriers of doubt, skepticism, and excuses. Embracing the truth of one's capabilities and aligning with a sense of purpose enables individuals to tap into their full potential. By embracing faith, acknowledging personal worth, and taking ownership of one's destiny, individuals can break free from the constraints of a survivalist mindset and unlock the greatness within themselves.

In conclusion, the failure to achieve one's potential is a significant consequence of a survivalist mindset. This occurs when individuals resist accepting the truth of their identity, question divine presence and power, and make excuses based on perceived limitations. To overcome this limitation, it is essential to embrace the truth of one's capabilities, have faith in divine guidance, and take ownership of one's destiny. By doing so, individuals can transcend the confines of a survivalist mindset and unleash their full potential, achieving greatness in their lives.

HOW IS A SURVIVALIST MINDSET DEVELOPED?

Proverbs 23:7 For as he thinketh in his heart, so is he...

The development of a survivalist mindset can be influenced by various factors, personal experiences, external circumstances, and even biological responses. Consider Gideon's position. At the time, the Israelites were subject to the Midianites for seven years. The Midianites were ruthless and carefree when it came to terrorizing the Israelites.

Understanding these factors can shed light on how individuals may react to challenging situations and adopt a survivalist mindset.

Read the following passage:

> **Judges 6:2** And the hand of Midian prevailed against Israel: and because of the Midianites the children of Israel made them the dens which are in the mountains, and caves, and strong holds. **3** And so it was, when Israel had sown, that the Midianites came up, and the Amalekites, and the children of the east, even they came up against them; **4** And they encamped against them, and destroyed the increase of the earth, till thou come unto Gaza, and left no sustenance for Israel, neither sheep, nor ox, nor ass. **5** For they came up with their cattle and their tents, and they came as grasshoppers for multitude; for both they and their camels were without number: and they entered into the land to destroy it.

Everything about the Midianites was destructive. The Israelites were at their mercy. There was nothing they could do. As a result, all they knew was how to survive. Or more correctly, they learned how to survive. That's right, survival is a learned behavior.

As a child, I grew up in an abusive household. As a result, my learned behavior was such that I learned to cope with what was going on. Each day was a journey in and of itself. Although I didn't realize it then, I was a survivalist. Just trying to make it through my "tough" terrain - or what I commonly called home.

Through my personal journey, I have come to understand that survival and coping are intertwined, and one of the most profound effects of surviving is the impact it has on our belief system. Our belief system becomes contaminated with our struggle, making us feel trapped and powerless in our daily lives. We begin to expect and look for what we have, and when we hear about an opportunity to escape, we act and think like it will never happen to me.

Our beliefs become our subconscious programming that not only directs our life but also controls our capacity for understanding and perception. This now subsequently becomes a survivalist mindset.

Our perception and understanding then keep us enslaved to the world we believe in and come to expect. So like Gideon, we'll thresh wheat in a winepress because we don't believe we can win. Thus hiding becomes our only natural choice.

But here's the truth: we were never created to live in failure or lack. Failure and lack go against every inherent instinct in man. Success and abundance are our natural state.

If we're going to change, we must be transformed by the power of God's Word.

The Lobster Effect

I came across an intriguing study that delves into the survivalist mentality, which is reflected through the behavior of lobsters.

These creatures inhabit the ocean floor and compete for limited territory, resulting in conflict and establishing a dominance hierarchy, also known as "The pecking order." Victorious lobsters secure the best locations, food, and mating opportunities through battles and victories, while others experience defeat and loss.

When a lobster is defeated in a battle, it undergoes a profound transformation. Its brain essentially dissolves, and a new subordinate brain grows. This new brain is more suitable for the lobster's lower position in the hierarchy. This remarkable adaptation demonstrates how the lobster's neural programming adjusts to its changed circumstances, from being a dominant individual to a subordinate one.

Like these lobsters, we, too, experience a similar transformation in our mindset after facing continuous defeat or adversity. Like Gideon, we too, may live in a survivalist mindset. We may lose confidence, feel threatened, and perceive ourselves as weak and anxious. The impact of repeated setbacks and challenges can reprogram our brains, leading to a pessimistic outlook and a focus on immediate survival rather than long-term growth and potential.

40 Days of Transformation

It is crucial to recognize how individuals react to these dark moments. They may lose their pride, lower their expectations, and show anxiety and insecurity. Some may become stuck in a state of defeat, resigning themselves to their lower status and lacking the energy or willingness to fight for a better outcome.

However, it is essential to remember that, unlike lobsters, humans can consciously reflect and choose. While a survivalist mindset may be a natural response to challenging circumstances, it does not have to be a permanent state. Individuals can actively work towards transforming their mindset, adopting a growth-oriented perspective, and reclaiming their confidence and determination.

Individuals can break free from the limitations of a survivalist mindset by cultivating resilience, seeking support, and embracing a mindset of possibility and self-belief. They can rewire their brains to focus on their potential, develop strategies for personal growth, and navigate challenges with resilience and optimism.

In conclusion, the development of a survivalist mindset can be influenced by personal experiences, external circumstances, and even biological responses. Understanding the factors contributing to this mindset allows us to explore how individuals may react to challenges and setbacks. By acknowledging the potential impact of defeat and adversity, individuals can consciously overcome a survivalist mindset, cultivate resilience, and embrace a growth-oriented perspective that unleashes their true potential.

TRANSITIONING FROM SURVIVING TO THRIVING

Until the pain of staying the same outweighs the pain of change, we will not change.   **- Tony Robbins**

When you're in survival, your prayer list is always larger than your praise list.

As we learned with Gideon, can you recall times when you've lived and spoken in similar terms, you were longing for escape or making excuses for your situation, and you couldn't hear or see the truth and possibilities in front of you? This limiting mindset keeps us trapped in a vicious survival cycle, stopping us from thriving. To break free from this pattern, we must let go of survival mode and embrace a mindset of faith and abundance.

> *The path of survival and thriving cannot be traveled at the same time.*

I have discovered some pointers that helped me evolve from surviving. It required me to shift my belief system or mindset from being steeped in hopelessness and lack to being restructured in hope and abundance.

 Here are some critical steps to take:

1. Acknowledge your current state.

> **Luke 15:17-19 -** "But when he came to himself, he said, 'How many of my father's hired servants have bread enough and to

spare, and I perish with hunger! **18.** I will arise and go to my father and will say to him, "Father, I have sinned against heaven and before you, **19.** and I am no longer worthy to be called your son. Make me like one of your hired servants." **20.** And he arose and came to his father. But when he was still a great way off, his father saw him and had compassion and ran and fell on his neck and kissed him.

This passage teaches about the Prodigal Son, who "came to himself" and realized his dire circumstances. His moment of reckoning wasn't about his physical location but his spiritual state.

Like the Prodigal Son, as long as we remain unaware of our struggles, we'll miss out on opportunities for growth and change.

Surviving and thriving do not run down the same road. To transition from surviving to thriving, we must look at where we are in our relationship with God. Otherwise, we will continue through life with blinders on.

The 17th verse highlights that the Prodigal Son "came to himself," which indicates he made a shift. This prompted his desire to transition from survival to thriving. It will be the same shift in us if we are to transition as well. Here's the truth of it: The path of survival and thriving cannot be traveled at the same time.

Acknowledging your current state, it will prevent you from wearing blinders. You'll remain oblivious to what's happening in your life. So, instead of taking charge in life, life happens to you. When life happens to you, you become accustomed to your circumstances. So much so that you don't realize other possibilities are available.

Recently, a colleague asked me how could I stand the smell from the athletic storage closet beside my office. I had grown so accustomed to the odor that I didn't notice it anymore. I replied, "I'm nose blind." She walked away in disgust that I'd become accustomed to a horrible smell.

The Prodigal Son recognized that he was in a state of "survival," out of money, working in a pig's pen, and eating pigs' food. He needed to return to his father's house. By acknowledging our spiritual state, we too, can take steps toward thriving.

2. Change the voice you're listening to.

John 10:27 - My sheep hear My voice, and I know them, and they follow Me.

God is always speaking! But are we always listening?

Adam and Eve in the Garden of Eden is a powerful reminder of the consequences of not heeding the voice of God. God created Adam and Eve in a perfect world, a garden filled with all they could ever need. Satan spoke to and tempted them in this garden, convincing them to eat from the Tree of Knowledge of Good and Evil, which God had forbidden.

They listened to the voice of the devil. They focused on a perception of lack instead of the voice of God, even though God had provided them with everything they needed. This act of disobedience led to a loss of innocence and the expulsion of Adam and Eve from the Garden of Eden.

The habits I created to survive will no longer serve me now that it's time to thrive.

This story serves as a warning to us today. We live in a world bombarding us with messages of lack, telling us that we need more and that we are not enough as we are. These messages can be so pervasive that we may not even realize we are listening to them.

The voice of God speaks of abundance and love, reminding us that we are enough as we are. It encourages us to trust in His provision and to have faith in Him. But, if we want to hear the voice of God, we must learn to discern the difference between His voice and the voice of lack.

Adam and Eve's disobedience led to their downfall. By tuning out the voice of lack and learning to listen to the voice of God, we can find peace and fulfillment. We can trust that He will provide for our needs and guide us on the path He has set for us. Our obedience to God's voice will lead to a life of abundance and joy.

If we are to hear His voice, it is essential to quiet our minds and listen for God's guidance. As Noah heard God's voice and followed His instructions, we too, can hear God's voice and follow His plan for our lives.

> **Genesis 6:22** - So Noah listened to God, and he built the ark. He did everything God asked him to do. [The Voice]

Known for being one of the most faithful servants of God in the Bible, Noah did as God instructed him by building an ark and gathering two of every kind of animal to prepare for a flood that would wipe out all living creatures on earth. Noah obeyed God's instruction without hesitation, despite the potential ridicule and disbelief of those around him.

Noah's unwavering faith is a testament to his deep connection with God. He could hear God's voice and follow His instructions without question. This ability to hear God's voice is not limited to Noah alone. As believers, we are all called and are well able to listen to and follow the voice of God.

Noah's obedience saved everyone on the ark, and also serves as a reminder of the importance of faith and obedience in our relationship with God. When we hear God's voice, we must trust and obey, even if it seems difficult or impossible.

3. Make a turn

Luke 15:18 - I will arise and go to my father, and will say to him, "Father, I have sinned against heaven and before you."

The prodigal son was willing to sacrifice living in a pig-pen to pursue something greater. To transition from surviving to thriving, it's crucial to make a turn and let go of the past. This is known as repentance, which involves changing our minds and committing to where we need to be.

Repentance may have religious connotations, but it means changing our mindset. Repentance means to turn from, acknowledging the need to let go of survival thinking and attitudes that hold us back. Letting go of our old ways and turning away from the mindset of just getting by is the first step.

Let's look at Romans 12:2.

Romans 12:2 - And do not be conformed to this world, but be transformed by the renewing of your mind, that you may prove what is that good and acceptable and perfect will of God.

We cannot stay where we are and expect things to change. Yet, so many people try. If your mind changes, you will change.

Acts 3:19 Repent therefore and be converted, that your sins may be blotted out, so that times of refreshing may come from the presence of the Lord,

This verse emphasizes that repentance and conversion go hand in hand. We turn from our old ways, seeking forgiveness and a fresh start, and we turn towards God's presence, ready to receive His blessings and experience times

Everything has to be converted from a negative to a positive.

of refreshing.

On the other hand, conversion means to turn towards. It's not just about leaving behind negative patterns; it's about embracing a new way of thinking and living. It's about turning towards thriving, growing, and fulfilling our potential.

To overcome failure, we need to shift our mindset towards positivity. By renewing our thoughts and transforming ourselves, we can become motivated by faith, belief, and success.

Finally, in Deuteronomy 2:3, the Children of Isreal were advised to turn northward and pursue something better. To move forward, we must let go of what no longer serves us and be ready to change.

New wine cannot go into old wineskins. We cannot contain the new things God wants to do if we are stuck in old mindsets.

Let's make the turn now and move towards new things.

4. Surround yourself with positive people

Surrounding yourself with positive influences is essential for transitioning from surviving to thriving. It means seeking out people who will encourage, uplift, and support you in your journey, whether joining a community of faith or seeking a mentor or coach, and surrounding yourself with positive people who share similar values and goals.

Proverbs 27:17 says, "As iron sharpens iron, so one person sharpens another." Just as two pieces of iron become sharper when rubbed together, we can become better versions of ourselves when we surround ourselves with positive influences. These people can challenge us to grow and push us toward our goals, helping us to thrive.

But, spending time with negative influences can have a detrimental effect. By sticking with negative people, we risk becoming stuck in the cycle of negativity and locking ourselves in survival mode. As Proverbs 13:20 says, "Walk with the wise and become wise, for a companion of fools suffers harm."

So, being intentional about the people you spend time with is essential.

5. Stop making excuses!

John 5:5 - Now a certain man was there who had an infirmity thirty-eight years. **6** When Jesus saw him lying there and knew that he had already been in that condition a long time, He said to him, "Do you want to be made well?" **7** The sick man answered Him, "Sir, I have no man to put me into the pool when the water is stirred up; but while I am coming, another step down before me." **8** Jesus said to him, "Rise, take up your bed, and walk." **9** And immediately, the man was made well, took up his bed, and walked.

We must take responsibility for the condition of our lives. And if we're going to transition from surviving to thriving, we cannot make excuses. People often use excuses to explain why they did something wrong—blaming external factors for their problems instead of taking responsibility for their actions. We must stop making excuses and become responsible for the condition of our lives.

I'm reminded of the sick man in John 5:5-9. Jesus asked him if he wanted to be well, and he responded by giving excuses for why he couldn't be healed. First, he blamed his lack of progress on having no one to help him; then, he blamed others for stepping in before him. But Jesus was not interested in his excuses; He wanted to know if the man wanted to be well.

If we, like this man, make excuses, we cannot move forward. We must take responsibility for our decisions and their consequences. We are the ones in control of our lives, not external circumstances. We must stop blaming others for our problems and take charge of our situations.

It's easy to fall into the trap of making excuses, blaming our lack of success on our upbringing, lack of resources, or whatever else. Yet, this mindset only keeps us in survival mode. It prevents us from taking the necessary steps to thrive and achieve our goals.

6. Trust the process

The journey from surviving to thriving can indeed be challenging. But it's important to remember that it requires patience, perseverance, and trust. These three qualities are essential to developing a strong and unwavering faith in God.

Patience is emphasized throughout the Bible. One of the most well-known verses on patience is in James 1:2-4, which says,

> **James 1:2-4 - 2** "Consider it pure joy, my brothers and sisters, whenever you face trials of many kinds, because you know that the testing of your faith produces perseverance. Let perseverance finish its work so you may be mature and complete, not lacking anything." Let's remember that difficult times can be growth opportunities. And that we should have patience as we endure trials.

Perseverance is another characteristic we must possess. Galatians 6:9 says, "Let us not become weary in doing good, for at the proper time we will reap a harvest if we do not give up." This verse encourages us to keep going even when tired or discouraged. We have to know that our efforts will be rewarded in due time.

Finally, trust is a vital component of our relationship with God. Proverbs 3:5-6 says, "Trust in the Lord with all your heart and lean not on your understanding; in all your ways submit to him, and he will make your paths straight." Here we are reminded to trust God's plan for our lives, even when we don't understand it. We can rely on His guidance and wisdom as we navigate life's challenges.

In the book of Psalms, we find the story of Joseph, a man who also went through a difficult process before he achieved his dreams. God gave Joseph a word, but until that Word was manifested, some testing and processing took place. Let's look at Psalm 105:19.

> **Psalm 105:19** Until the time that his Word came to pass, The Word of the Lord tested him.

Look at what the New Living Translation says,

> **Psalm 105:19** Until the time came to fulfill his dreams, the Lord tested Joseph's character. [NLT]

This testing was necessary to prepare Joseph for his incredible destiny. So, if you're in the midst of a difficult season or what seems to be a holding pattern, remember that it's a sign that you're still on the journey to fulfilling your dreams.

When we desire to transition, we, too, will have to go through those times of "testing" before our dreams are fulfilled.

But what do you do when you feel you can't go on? When the challenges are seen as insurmountable, and the finish line feels impossibly far away? That's when you need to hold on to your faith and remember the words of the apostle Paul in Philippians 3:12:

> **Phil. 3:12** I'm not there yet, nor have I become perfect; but I am charging on to gain anything and everything the Anointed One, Jesus, has in store for me—and nothing will stand in my way because He has grabbed me and won't let me go. [VOICE]

Even though Paul hadn't yet reached his goal, he knew to continue that he would be on his way and that he would not be deterred by any obstacle that came his way.

Similarly, you must also press on toward your goals and trust that nothing will stand in your way as long as you keep moving forward. Please don't give up, no matter how tough it gets. Keep pressing on toward your dreams, and remember that all things are possible with God on your side.

Isaiah 58:6-11 - 6 Is not this the fast that I have chosen? To loose the bands of wickedness, to undo the heavy burdens, and to let the oppressed go free, and that ye break every yoke?

WHAT IS THE DANIEL FAST?

Daniel 1:8 But Daniel resolved that he would not defile himself with the king's food or with the wine that he drank. Therefore he asked the chief of the eunuchs to allow him not to defile himself."

The Daniel Fast is a Biblical-based partial fast often performed for 21 days (though 10-day and 40-day fasts are also common). It's meant to be a cleansing for the body and to enhance spiritual health by simplifying your diet. The goal of the fast is not to lose weight but to draw closer to God.

Daniel Fast recipes are plant-based, with no bread or sweeteners. There are two passages (Daniel 1:12 and Daniel 10:12-13) that define the diet as:
- Eating only fruits, vegetables, legumes, whole grains, nuts, and seeds
- Avoiding "choice foods" such as meat, dairy, and sugars
- Drinking only water

Why Are You Fasting?

In the Bible, fasting is often associated with repentance, seeking God's guidance, and mourning. In the Old Testament, fasting was a way to humble oneself before God, to show sorrow for sin, and to seek forgiveness and restoration of relationship with God. In the New Testament, Jesus fasted for 40 days in the wilderness before beginning his ministry, and he taught his followers about the importance of fasting as a spiritual discipline.

Biblical fasting is not just about abstaining from food but also about turning away from sin and focusing on God. It is a way to draw closer to God and to seek his will in one's life. Through fasting, believers demonstrate their dependence on God and willingness to sacrifice their fleshly desires to seek God's presence and guidance. Fasting is required to deepen one's relationship with God and seek his will in one's life, not a way to earn His favor.

Make Your Commitment

Participating in our 40-day devotional can be a powerful way to grow spiritually and deepen your relationship with God.

1. **Set aside time:** Commit to setting aside a specific time each day to participate in the devotional. It's essential to make this a priority and schedule it into your day to be consistent. Here are some steps to help you make your commitment:

2. **Choose a quiet space:** Find a quiet area to focus and avoid distractions. This may be a specific room in your home or a quiet corner in a park. Wherever you choose, make sure it's a place where you can be comfortable and relaxed.

3. **Create accountability:** Share your commitment to the 40-day devotional with a friend or family member, and ask them to hold you accountable. This can help you stay motivated and committed even when you face challenges.

4. **Engage fully in the devotional:** When participating in the devotional, be fully engaged and present. Read each day's material carefully, meditate on the scripture, and pray. Try to apply what you learn to your daily life.

5. **Reflect on your experience:** Reflect on your experience with the devotional. Consider what you've learned, how you've grown, and what changes you'd like to make due to your participation.

WHAT CAN YOU EAT ON THE DANIEL FAST?

On the Daniel Fast, you eat plant-based meals that are nutritious and delicious while setting aside other foods as an act of worship and sacrifice to the Lord.

The following list explains the categories of foods and foods to avoid on the Daniel Fast. Remember that the list below is not all-inclusive, and not all items are listed here.

SPECIAL NOTE: Most Daniel Fasts exclude eating meat. However, for this devotional, we'll allow some lean meat: Chicken, turkey, and seafood. What's important is never to overindulge and eat in excess.

Daniel Fast food list

- **Whole grains:** Barley, brown rice, buckwheat, farro, millet, oats, popcorn, quinoa, rice cakes, rye, sorghum, whole wheat, whole-wheat pasta, and wild rice.
- **Beans and legumes:** Black beans, black-eyed peas, cannellini beans, garbanzo beans (chickpeas), great northern beans, kidney beans, lentils, peanuts, pinto beans, and split peas.
- **Nuts and seeds:** Almonds, cashews, hazelnuts, macadamia nuts, natural nut butter (no additives), peanuts, pecans, pumpkin seeds, pine nuts, pistachios, poppy seeds, sesame seeds, soy nuts, sunflower seeds, and walnuts.
- **Vegetables:** All vegetables, whether fresh, frozen, dried, juiced, or canned.
- **Fruits:** All fruit, whether fresh, frozen, dried, juiced, or canned (so long as it doesn't contain added sugar).
- **Oils:** Oils can be used minimally but not for deep-frying.
- **Herbs, spices, and seasonings:** Includes salt and pepper.
- **Soy products:** All soy products, including tofu.
- **Unleavened bread:** Whole-grain bread made without yeast, sugars, or preservatives.
- **Water:** Distilled, filtered, sparkling, spring, and mineral waters allowed.

- **100-percent fruit juice:** Natural, 100-percent fruit juice is allowed but should be had sparingly.
- **Meat**: Chicken, turkey, and seafood (non-scavenger)
- **Wraps** (flour) are acceptable in light amounts.

All soy protein products are good, as well as Oatmeal, Creme of Wheat, and Grits (in fair moderation)

Things to avoid on the Daniel Fast
- **Animal products:** All red meat, pork, scavenger seafood, and crustaceans.
- **Sweeteners:** Agave nectar, artificial sweeteners, brown rice syrup, brown sugar, cane juice, corn syrup, honey, malt syrup, molasses, raw sugar, sugar, and other syrups.
- **Leavened bread:** Bread made with yeast.
- **Refined and processed foods:** Foods that contain artificial flavorings, artificial preservatives, food additives, white flour, and white rice.
- **Deep-fried foods:** All fried foods.
- **Solid fats:** Butter, lard, margarine, and shortening.
- **Chocolate:** Milk chocolate, semi-sweet chocolate, dark chocolate, chocolate syrup, and cacao.
- **Some beverages:** Alcohol, coffee, and other caffeinated beverages.
- **No Dairy products.**

PREPARATION

Before the fast
1. Drink a lot of water: squeeze fresh lemon juice into your water.
2. Begin to decrease your caffeine and sugar intake. Drinking a lot of water will help you overcome cravings for these two items.

WHY 40 DAYS?

Personal growth and transformation don't happen suddenly or instantly but are relatively gradual, requiring discipline, effort, and patience. The number 40 holds great significance in the Bible and appears multiple times throughout the Old and New Testaments. It is often used to symbolize testing, trial, or waiting period. From Noah's flood, when it rained for 40 days and 40 nights, to Moses spending 40 days and 40 nights on Mount Sinai receiving the Ten Commandments, the end of each signified that the person had undergone a significant transformation: even Jesus was tempted by the devil for 40 days in the wilderness just before starting his ministry.

40 Days of Transformation is a period of transition and growth, spiritual transformation and preparation, during which individuals strive to better themselves and their relationship with God. This transformation period is a means to move from one state of being to another, often to thrive in a new and improved way.

FASTING SCHEDULE

During the 40 days, the two fasting concepts utilized are full and partial fasts. A complete fast involves abstaining from all food and drink, except water, for a fixed period. A partial fast limits one's intake of specific foods and reduces consumption.

Full and partial fasts can have spiritual, physical, and emotional benefits, depending on the person and the reason for fasting. Complete fasts can help to increase spiritual focus, detoxify the body, and promote weight loss, while partial fasts can improve digestion, boost energy levels, and provide a sense of discipline.

Below is the eating schedule we'll use. To maximize your experience, follow the plan as closely as possible.

40 Days of Transformation

DAY	TIME	FOOD SCHEDULE
Mon - Tue. - Thur. - Fri.	6:00 am - 8:00 pm	FOODS FROM LIST
Wednesday *	6:00 am - 6:00 pm	FULL FAST
Saturday	6:00 am - 12:00 pm	FULL FAST
	12:00 pm - 8:00	FOODS FROM LIST
Sunday	6:00 am - 8:00 pm	FREE DAY**

* On Wednesday you can eat from 6 pm - 8 pm.

** Free Days - not on a fasting schedule. Adhere to no red meat, pork, scavenger seafood, and crustaceans instructions.

It's important to note that fasting should only be undertaken by consulting a healthcare professional, especially if you have any underlying health conditions. Additionally, it's recommended to gradually work up to more extended fasting periods and break a fast gradually rather than abruptly.

WHY MAKE DECLARATIONS?

Job 22.28   You will also declare a thing, And it will be established for you; So light will shine on your ways.

God's Word has the power to change our lives. Through reading the Bible, we grow in faith, and our spirit, soul, and body are refreshed and revived. Similarly, when we daily make biblical declarations, we further open ourselves to hearing God's Word and experiencing its transformative power. As the Scripture tells us, faith comes by hearing and hearing the Word of God.

In a world filled with negativity and chaos, it's easy to be overwhelmed by fear, doubt, and discouragement. However, the Bible teaches us that our words have power. Making biblical declarations can help to align our thoughts and words with God's truth. By speaking God's truth over our lives, we can shift our perspective and focus on His promises instead of our problems. As we declare God's truth, our mind and heart are unified, and we can experience the peace and joy that comes from trusting in Him.

> Biblical declarations align our thoughts and words with God's truth

Making biblical declarations is also a way of exercising our faith. Having faith is essential in our Christian walk because, without faith, it's impossible to please God (Hebrews 11:6). When we declare God's promises, we put our faith into action. We choose to believe that God's Word is accurate and that He is faithful to fulfill His promises.

Making biblical declarations is a way of speaking life into our circumstances. The Bible teaches us that death and life are in the power of the tongue (Proverbs 18:21). Our words have the power to create or destroy, to encourage or discourage, to uplift or tear down. So, instead of speaking defeat and negativity, we are speaking God's truth and declaring His goodness over our lives and victory over our struggles.

Making biblical declarations is also a way of inviting God's presence and power into our lives. The Bible teaches us that God inhabits the praises of His people (Psalm 22:3). As we make biblical declarations, we praise God for who He is and what He has done.

Making biblical declarations is a powerful tool for transforming our lives. By aligning our thoughts and words with God's truth, exercising our faith, speaking life into and over our circumstances, and inviting God's presence and power into our lives, we can experience the abundant life that God has promised us.

For the next 40 days, we will make daily declarations based on biblical principles that align with Spirit-led goals and aspirations, which lead us to thrive.

THE POWER OF THRIVING

The righteous flourish like the palm tree,
Their leaves evergreen, forever free,
In grace and truth they grow and stand,
A witness to the Master's hand.

Their roots are firm, in soil deep,
Their branches high, they do not weep,
And in each season, come what may,
Their fruit abounds, both night and day.

They drink the rain, the dew, the sun,
Their strength and beauty, ever won,
And in the courts of God they sing,
Forevermore, their praises ring.

For He has planted them with care,
In holy ground, He's placed them there,
To flourish, grow, and bear much fruit,
And bring Him glory, love, and truth.

So let us be like palms, ever strong,
In faith, in love, in grace, lifelong,
And let our lives, like branches, sway,
In praise to God, both night and day.

-Lane Hawkins

1. WE WERE CREATED TO THRIVE

Psalm 92:12-14 - 12 The righteous shall flourish like a palm tree, He shall grow like a cedar in Lebanon. **13** Those who are planted in the house of the Lord shall flourish in the courts of our God. **14** They shall still bear fruit in old age; They shall be fresh and flourishing,

This week, we focus on the truth that God created us to thrive. God is a God of abundance, not lack, and our lives should reflect His abundance. It's in our spiritual DNA.

To thrive, we must recognize who we are in Christ, see ourselves as God sees us, and live up to that reality. We must be confident and rooted in His love for us. This empowers us to pursue our dreams, overcome our fears, and live in a way that honors Him.

Thriving also means being rooted in God's presence. Like a tree needs water and nutrients to grow, we need nourishment from God's

Word and His presence to thrive. Spending time with Him refreshes and strengthens us to live out His purpose.

We may face obstacles that seek to hinder our growth and prevent us from thriving. Fear, doubt, sin, and past wounds can hold us back, but God promises to be with us and help us overcome these obstacles. We can rely on His strength to experience the fullness of life He desires.

So, let us open our hearts and minds to all God has in store for us this week. These daily devotionals will guide us to understand that we were created to thrive as God intended. May they be a source of encouragement, inspiration, and growth as we seek to thrive in every aspect of our lives.

DAY 1 - WE WERE CREATED TO THRIVE

Psalm 92:12-14 - *12 The righteous shall flourish like a palm tree, He shall grow like a cedar in Lebanon. 13 Those who are planted in the house of the Lord Shall flourish in the courts of our God. 14   They shall still bear fruit in old age; They shall be fresh and flourishing,*

God has given us everything we need to thrive. In the above passage, the writer compares us to the Bible's two most talked about trees: the palm and cedar.

Known for its resilience and ability, the palm tree can thrive in harsh conditions. It can withstand strong winds and intense heat and still grow tall and strong.

Like the palm, as believers, we thrive even amid difficult circumstances as long as we remain rooted in His Word and presence.

Strength and durability are the characteristics of the cedar tree. We obtain these characteristics as our relationship with God grows. We become steadfast and unshakable, able to withstand the storms of life. Our roots grow deep, anchored in the truth of God's Word. And as we stay connected to Him, we bear fruit that brings glory to His name.

So, let us be like the palm and the cedar trees, rooted in the house of the Lord and flourishing in His courts. Trust in His faithfulness and steadfast love, and may we bear fruit that brings glory to His name. May we thrive in every season of life, knowing that our God is with us and will sustain us through it all.

DECLARATION
I am made to prosper and flourish in every area of my life.

DAY 2 - WE WERE CREATED TO THRIVE

Psalm 1.3 *He shall be like a tree Planted by the rivers of water That brings forth its fruit in its season, Whose leaf also shall not wither; And whatever he does shall prosper.*

What a fitting visualization. The believer is like a prosperous and fruitful tree that someone planted by the waters.

Again, we are compared to a tree. When our foundation in life is in God, we will prosper no matter what happens or what we go through.

Being planted by streams of water is a key to thriving. As a tree needs water to grow and flourish, we, too, need to stay connected to our source of life, God our Father. How do we do this? We do it by spending time in His presence, His Word, and in prayer. As we abide in His presence, we find ourselves refreshed and nourished, bearing fruit that brings Him glory.

The verse also tells us that the tree yields its fruit in season. This means there is a time for everything, and we must be patient and trust God's timing. We must take our time with the process of growth and maturity.

Like the cedar, the fact that the tree's leaf does not wither is a testament to its strength and resilience. We are withstanding the storms of life and remaining steadfast in our faith. We can be confident that our God is with us and will sustain us.

Finally, the verse tells us that whatever the tree does prospers. It's clear that we will go through trials and tribulations, but when we live according to His will and purpose, we will experience His favor and blessing.

So, let us be like the tree planted by rivers of water, thriving and flourishing. Let us stay connected to the source of life, bearing fruit and remaining strong and resilient. And may all that we do prosper, bringing glory to God and blessing those around us.

DECLARATION
I will flourish like a well-watered tree, rooted and established in Christ.

DAY 3 - WE WERE CREATED TO THRIVE

Deuteronomy 28.3-6 - *3* *"Blessed shall you be in the city, and blessed shall you be in the country. **4** "Blessed shall be the fruit of your body, the produce of your ground and the increase of your herds, the increase of your cattle and the offspring of your flocks.* ***5*** *"Blessed shall be your basket and your kneading bowl.* ***6*** *"Blessed shall you be when you come in, and blessed shall you be when you go out.*

We must renew our minds to the idea that I am blessed. I've said, "I'm not looking for a blessing; I live in the blessing." Our concept of a blessing is limited to things. If we get a new car, we shout, "God blessed me with my new car!" We make the car the blessing. But instead of making the car the reason we are blessed, we have to learn to understand that "I have a new car because I am blessed!" I am blessed, so I get the car, not I got the car, so I'm blessed.

Deut. 28 paints this beautifully: We are blessed! What a promise. And this promise is simple. As we trust Him, we can expect to see those blessings manifested in our lives. God has blessed us whether we live in the city or the country. He has blessed our children, our livelihoods, and our daily provision.

It's essential to remember that we are not blessed for our benefit. As we thrive, we must be a blessing to others. We are to use our gifts, resources, and abilities to help those in need, share the gospel, and serve our communities with love and compassion.

DECLARATION
I am blessed in the city, blessed in the field, and blessed in everything I do.

DAY 4 - WE WERE CREATED TO THRIVE

Psalm 128:2 *You will eat the fruit of your labor; blessings and prosperity will be yours. [NIV]*

As individuals who hold firm in our faith, our purpose is to flourish and live a life that brings honor to God. It can be tempting to associate thriving solely with material possessions, believing that the more possessions we accumulate, the more prosperous we become. However, true thriving and prosperity encompass far more than mere material wealth.

By placing our trust in the Lord and faithfully adhering to His commandments, we position ourselves for genuine success. Embracing a life centered on God's guidance and principles enables us to experience fulfillment and true prosperity.

Prosperity and success are to touch all aspects of our lives, including our relationships, health, spiritual growth, and emotional well-being. It's God's desire for us to thrive, and he has promised that the works of our hands will be blessed.

Remember, our prosperity and thriving don't depend on our efforts or abilities. It's by God's grace and favor. Thus, let us commit ourselves to walk in His ways and trust His blessing.

Remember that true prosperity is not only about what we can gain for ourselves.   It's about how we can use our blessing to bless others. As we thrive, let's seek to bless those around us and use our gifts to further God's kingdom.

DECLARATION
My work is blessed with abundance, and my yield will always be increased.

DAY 5 - WE WERE CREATED TO THRIVE

John 15.5 *I am the vine, you are the branches. He who abides in Me, and I in him, bears much fruit; for without Me, you can do nothing.*

Thriving is not surviving, and surviving is not thriving.

Thriving is about flourishing and growing. It's experiencing the fullness of life that Jesus promised us. To thrive, we must stay connected to Jesus like the branches need to stay connected to the vine.

What does it mean to Abide in Jesus? It's about spending time with Him, reading His Word, praying, and seeking His guidance. It means trusting Him and relying on Him for everything we need. It also means obeying His commands and living according to His will.

When we remain in Jesus, we can bear much fruit (fruit production is akin to thriving). Fruitfulness is a sign of a healthy and thriving relationship with Jesus.

Apart from Jesus, we can do nothing. It's only in Jesus can we find the abundant life we were created to experience.

As we strive to thrive, remember to stay connected to Jesus, the true vine. Let us abide in Him and allow Him to produce fruit in us. Let us trust in His plan for our lives and follow His lead. When we do, we will experience the fullness of life that He promised us and thrive in every aspect of our lives.

DECLARATION
I declare that I am fruitful and productive in all that I do.

DAY 6 - WE WERE CREATED TO THRIVE

WEEKLY DECLARATIONS

Take this time to make the declarations we've made throughout the week.

I am made to prosper and flourish in every area of my life.

I will flourish like a well-watered tree, rooted and established in Christ.

I am blessed in the city, blessed in the field, and blessed in everything I do.

My work is blessed with abundance, and my yield will always be increased.

I declare that I am fruitful and productive in all that I do.

DAY 7 - WE WERE CREATED TO THRIVE

ACTIVATION

Jeremiah 30:2 *Thus speaks the Lord God of Israel, saying: 'Write in a book for yourself all the words that I have spoken to you.*

Take some time to write what God has spoken to you this week. What areas do you need to change, and what steps will you take to make those changes?

_____

_____

_____

_____

_____

_____

_____

_____

_____

_____

_____

_____

_____

_____

_____

THE POWER OF FORGIVENESS

To forgive is to release the weight,
Of anger, hurt, and bitter hate,
It's choosing love above all else,
And letting go of what was once felt.

It's a step towards a brighter day,
Where grace and mercy have a say,
And in forgiveness, we can find,
A way to heal and free our mind.

- Lane Hawkins

2. THE PRINCIPLE OF RELEASE

J*ohn 20:22-23* - *22 And with that he breathed on them and said, "Receive the Holy Spirit. **23** If you forgive anyone's sins, their sins are forgiven; if you do not forgive them, they are not forgiven."*

Everyone who has ever lived has been offended. Not once, but multiple times. In some cases, numerous times. In Luke 17:1, the Bible unequivocally states that offenses must occur. But we're not to live our lives based on offenses or allow ourselves to lock us into a life of bondage and oppression because

> **Colossians 1:13** *He has delivered us from the power of darkness and conveyed us into the kingdom of the Son of His love, **14** in whom we have redemption through His blood, the forgiveness of sins.*

we've been offended. Christ died to release us from the pains and limitations of this world.

The definition of release is to allow or enable escape from confinement, to be set free.

The Principle of Release is about letting go of things that hold us back and impede our progress.

As we read in John 20.23, we see an excellent concept introduced by Jesus; if you forgive anyone's sins, their sins are forgiven; if you do not forgive their sins, they are not forgiven." I like to state it this way:

What I hold on to, I hold on to; what I let go of, I let go of.

This sounds simplistic and even elementary. And yet, I believe the truth is liberating.

Luke 17:1 says, "offenses will come," but our problem isn't with the coming offense. Our problem lies in how we handle it. Do we hold on to it, or do we let it go?

To thrive to the level God desires, we must learn to flow and function in the Principle of Release.

Let me give it to you one more time:

What I hold on to, I hold on to; what I let go of, I let go of.

Philippians 4:8 Finally, brethren, whatever things are true, whatever things are noble, whatever things are just, whatever things are pure, whatever things are lovely, whatever things are of good report, if there is any virtue and if there is anything praiseworthy—meditate on these things. This reminds us to be deliberate about what we retain and what we release. Negative emotions such as false judgment, anger, bitterness, and resentment are toxic and will stifle our growth and lead to bitterness and resentment, ultimately leading us to survival mode.

Instead of holding on to these destructive emotions, we should let them go and concentrate on positive things, such as forgiveness, love, and peace.

We reap numerous benefits when we release things that hold us back. Hebrews 12 says we are to put away every weight and sin that easily ensnares us.

While letting go is vital to achieving personal growth and realizing our full potential, it can be difficult. It requires courage and determination to release the things that weigh us down, but in doing so, we create space for new opportunities and experiences that can lead to a more fulfilling life.

DAY 8 - THE PRINCIPLE OF RELEASE

Ephesians 4.32 *And be kind to one another, tenderhearted, forgiving one another, even as God in Christ forgave you.*

Have you ever considered thriving in our relationships? It's not something that is usually put together. But this is a significant aspect of what forgiveness is about.

Jesus teaches that we are to love our neighbor as ourselves. And when we forgive, that's exactly what we're doing. We're showing love for ourselves by letting go of our hurts, pains, and offenses. And we're showing love for our "neighbor" by releasing them from our judgment. This allows us to build healthy, strong, and meaningful connections. Thus we are thriving.

Kindness and compassion are essential ingredients in any thriving relationship. When we show kindness, we are extending grace and generosity. When we show compassion, we are demonstrating empathy and understanding. Kindness and compassion working together generate tremendous power; that's undeniable. We are creating a safe and nurturing environment allowing everyone to flourish and grow.

Everyone makes mistakes. But, when we quickly forgive, we create space for healing and reconciliation. Forgiveness allows us to move beyond our hurts and offenses.

We understand how much God loves us, and we can love others similarly. Showing kindness, compassion, and forgiveness is found through our experience of God's grace. And recognizing how much we are forgiven empowers us to extend that same forgiveness to others.

Thriving in our relationships requires effort and intentionality. Let's not slack in showing kindness, compassion, and forgiveness. They are the currency of thriving relationships.

DECLARATION
I am filled with compassion and kindness, and I choose to forgive those who have hurt me just as Christ forgave me.

DAY 9 - THE PRINCIPLE OF RELEASE

Psalm 119:165 *Great peace have they which love thy law: and nothing shall offend them.*

I know we've all had this happen. You're walking down the street, minding your business, when bam! Your foot hits a deep crack in the pavement, and you lose your balance. You stumbled. Hopefully, you avoided falling and hitting the pavement, and no one saw it. You avoided being some meme on social media.

Stumbling only happens because we're walking. We're making progress. We're not in the same place. For many, the fear of stumbling in our journey prohibits our movement. We're afraid to stumble, so we don't move at all. I have never heard of someone "stumbling" while sitting down.

Peace is the byproduct of loving God's Word and aligning our lives with his plans and purposes. And as a result of peace, we can become "stumble-proof."

Usually, stumbling is a direct result of something we didn't see: the crack, the tree root, the shoe in the dark, or whatever. Our attention was somewhere else. But through the Word of God, we can gain the focus and clarity we need to avoid life's stumbling blocks.

Through the Word of God, we gain the wisdom to handle life's challenges. We acquire the courage and ability to take risks and go beyond our comfort zone to fulfill God's purpose. We can recognize the traps and snares that the enemy lays before us—becoming better equipped to resist temptation and overcome adversity.

DECLARATION
I have the great Peace of God in my life by His word, and nothing shall offend me.

DAY 10 - THE PRINCIPLE OF RELEASE

Hebrews 12:15 *looking carefully lest anyone fall short of the grace of God; lest any root of bitterness springing up cause trouble, and by this, many become defiled;*

Bitterness is a toxic emotion. It will take root in our hearts when we feel wronged or hurt. Allowing unresolved pain and disappointment to fester will consume and poison us.

Joseph is a wonderful example for us. He was someone whose life was overwhelmed with tragedy. But he refused to choose the way of bitterness. He chose a more powerful way. The method of forgiveness. He did not allow bitterness to suck the life out of him nor keep him from his destiny.

As believers, we have to forgive others as we have been forgiven. But forgiveness is not always easy, especially when we are hurt. We must let go of our anger, resentment, and bitterness and extend grace and love to those who have wronged us.

A key to overcoming bitterness is to fix our eyes on Jesus and trust in His promises. When we focus on His love and grace, we will find the strength and courage to forgive others, even when it seems impossible. We will also find healing and wholeness for our wounded hearts as we release our pain and hurt to Him.

One way to cultivate a heart of forgiveness is to practice gratitude. Focus on the blessings in our lives rather than the hurts and injustices. We will find peace and joy in our struggles by shifting our perspective and seeing things differently.

Forgiveness is a choice that we must make, even when it feels difficult or unfair. We must let go of our bitterness and extend grace and love to others as we have received from Christ.

By holding onto bitterness, we will impede our ability to thrive. Look at this passage:

> **Job 21:25** - Another man dies in the bitterness of his soul, Never having eaten with pleasure.

Bitterness is the ultimate poison! But thankfully, through forgiveness, we have the ultimate antidote.

DECLARATION
I will not let bitterness take root in my heart but choose forgiveness and let go of anger and resentment.

DAY 11 - THE PRINCIPLE OF RELEASE

Isaiah 43:18 *Do not remember the former things, Nor consider the things of old.* **19** *Behold, I will do a new item, Now it shall spring forth; Shall you not know it? I will even make a road in the wilderness And rivers in the desert.*

The way of God is to start fresh.

In the famous movie, "The Lion King," Simba has a powerful and moving moment. He has the revelation that his dad lives on in him and that he has been hiding from his past. This is the turning point in the movie.

Simba, who is burdened with guilt from the role he felt he played in his father's death, is having a conversation with Rafiki — the wise old baboon!

They talk about how change is good, but it takes work. Simba says that returning means facing his past, and he has been running from it for so long.

Rafiki — then hits Simba with a stick on the head!! When Simba asks him, "What was that for?" He replies, "Doesn't matter — it's in the past."

Simba then says, "Yes, but it still hurts." Rafiki replies with his key message " —Ah yes; the past can hurt. But the way I see it, you can either run from it or learn from it."

When I coached High School football, I always talked about being present. It was one of the seven pillars I built the program on. Those seven pillars were: Brotherhood, Effort, Leadership, Integrity, Engage the moment (be present), Vision and Endurance. This form the acrostic: BELIEVE.
It's easy to check out, of where we are and look for a way of escape. Whether is by drugs, alcohol, over working or anything for that

matter provides a means of escape, we find ourselves in survival mode. But, by staying present, being in the moment, we can hold true to who we are.

As we go through life, it is easy to be distracted. But by being present, we remain conscious of who we are. This is where our power and abilities lie.

Christians are called to live in the present and look to the future with hope and faith. We are not defined by our past but by God's grace and love, which has redeemed us and given us a new identity in Christ.

Moving forward can be challenging and tricky, especially when we have experienced deep pain, trauma, or loss. When we let our past lock us down, we carry the weight of all those years of pain. And no matter how hard we try, we can't seem to lift it off. In these moments, it's important to remember that we are not alone. God is with us. Jesus said, "Come to Me, all *you* who labor and are heavy laden, and I will give you rest." What a promise! He promises to give us the courage and wisdom to face each day with hope and confidence, no matter what may come.

By holding on to the past, we hold on to bitterness, resentment, or unforgiveness. We only hurt ourselves and hinder our growth and healing, thrusting us into survival mode.

We can move forward when we focus on the present. We can ask God for wisdom and guidance and take small daily steps toward our goals and dreams.

So let us take these words to heart. Let's choose to forget the former things and not dwell on the past. Trust God's promises and live daily with hope, faith, and love. Let's move forward with courage, forgiveness, and purpose. Following his leading and thriving in the abundant life he has given us.

"Ah yes, the past can hurt. But the way I see it, you can either run from it or learn from it."

DECLARATION
I am letting go of past hurt, pain, and resentment. I choose to forgive and move forward, trusting God's healing and restoring power.

DAY 12 - THE PRINCIPLE OF RELEASE

Colossians 3:15 *And let the peace of God rule in your hearts, to which also you were called in one body; and be thankful.*

We sang an old Chorus song from Maranatha Music over 30 years ago. It's entitled: He is our peace:

He is our peace
Who has broken down every wall,
He is our peace; He is our peace.
He is our peace
Who has broken down every wall,
He is our peace; He is our peace.

Cast all your cares on Him,
For He cares for you,
He is our peace; He is our peace.

We are to live in peace.

You and I know living in peace with one another can be challenging, especially in a world with division, conflict, and discord.

As the body of Christ, it's our responsibility to love and support one another. Even when we disagree or have different opinions or perspectives. We are to seek unity in Christ and to let his peace rule in our hearts.

But what does it look like "to seek unity?" We have to learn to listen to one another. And listen with all sincerity. That means we are to listen so we can understand and learn. But often, we only listen to respond. This will lead us to a dead end. We are to listen with an open heart. Be empathetic, not only sympathetic. Put yourself in someone else's shoes.

It means being willing to put aside our desires and agendas.   But look to build up the body of Christ and fulfill His purposes.

We can trust God's goodness and sovereignty and rely on his strength and wisdom. When we allow the peace of Christ to rule in our hearts, we are transformed from the inside out. We experience a sense of calm, contentment, and joy in the face of life's challenges and struggles.

And when we cultivate an attitude of gratitude, we will see God's faithfulness and provision in our lives. We will see the blessings all around us. We will be thankful for the people in our lives and our opportunities. God is working in and through us.

So strive to let the peace of Christ rule in your heart and be thankful for all that He is doing. Let us seek to live in peace with one another and build up Christ's body through our words and actions. Let's trust His promises and rely on His strength. Let's seek to fulfill His purposes and thrive in the abundant life He has given us.

DECLARATION
I will let the peace of Christ rule in my heart, and I will be thankful, forgiving others in love, as Christ has forgiven me.

DAY 13 - THE PRINCIPLE OF RELEASE
WEEKLY DECLARATIONS

Take this time to make the declarations we've made throughout the week.

I am filled with compassion and kindness, and I choose to forgive those who have hurt me just as Christ forgave me.

I have the great Peace of God in my life by His word, and nothing shall offend me.

I will not let bitterness take root in my heart but choose forgiveness and let go of anger and resentment.

I am letting go of past hurt, pain, and resentment. I choose to forgive and move forward, trusting God's healing and restoring power.

I will let the peace of Christ rule in my heart, and I will be thankful, forgiving others in love, as Christ has forgiven me.

DAY 14 - THE PRINCIPLE OF RELEASE

ACTIVATION

Jeremiah 30:2 *Thus speaks the Lord God of Israel, saying: 'Write in a book for yourself all the words that I have spoken to you.*

Take some time to write what God has spoken to you this week. What areas do you need to change, and what steps will you take to make those changes?

THE PROMISE OF THE HARVEST

Every seed we sow into the ground,
Holds a promise that's waiting to be found,
For in due time, with sun and rain,
A harvest comes, and we reap again.

With careful hands, we plant the seed,
And tend the soil with utmost heed,
We watch and wait as days go by,
And hope and pray for fruit to arise.

But sowing isn't just a simple task,
It's a commitment that we must ask,
For every seed needs time and care,
To grow and flourish, beyond compare.

And when the harvest time has come,
We see the fruits of what we've done,
We reap what we have sown and grown,
And give thanks to God for all He's shown.

So let us sow with generous hands,
And trust the work of God's commands,
For in the sowing and the reaping,
We find a joy that's truly worth keeping.

- Lane Hawkins

3. THE PRINCIPLE OF HARVEST

From the seeds I sow, a harvest will grow.

Genesis 8:22 While the earth remains, seedtime and harvest, cold and heat, winter and summer, and day and night shall not cease.

This week, our study will take us on a journey through the principle of harvest as we explore 2 Corinthians 9:6, which states: "Remember this: Whoever sows sparingly will also reap sparingly, and whoever sows generously will also reap generously."

The concept of sowing and reaping is a fundamental principle throughout the Bible, and it has significant implications for our lives as Christians. This principle reminds us that we will reap what we sow, good or bad. If we sow generously, we can expect to reap bountifully, but if we sow sparingly, we will reap sparingly. In essence, we will reap what we sow; and we will reap how we sow.

Galatians 6:7 Do not be deceived; God is not mocked; for whatever a man sows, that he will also reap.

1 Cor. 9:6 He that sows sparingly will reap sparingly...

As we delve deeper into this passage, it's important to note that the principle of harvest is not just about giving financially, although that is undoubtedly one aspect of it. When we give generously, we can expect to receive blessings in return.

> *The seed you sow, will leave your present and enter into your future and await for your arrival.*

This principle applies to every area of our lives, including our time, talents, and treasures.

In Galatians 6:7-9, Paul emphasizes this principle when he says: "Do not be deceived: God cannot be mocked. A man reaps what he sows. Whoever sows to please their flesh, from the flesh, will reap destruction; whoever sows to please the Spirit, from the Spirit, will reap eternal life. Let us not become weary in doing good, for at the proper time, we will reap a harvest if we do not give up."

In this passage, we see that the principle of harvest extends beyond this life and into eternity. If we sow to please our flesh, we will reap destruction, but if we sow to please the Spirit, we will reap eternal life. This is a reminder that our actions have consequences, both in this life and the next.

The principle of harvest also teaches us about stewardship. In Luke 16:10-11, Jesus says: "Whoever can be trusted with very little can also be trusted with much, and whoever is dishonest with very little will also be dishonest with much. So who will trust you with true riches if you have not been trustworthy in handling worldly wealth?"

As we reflect on this passage, we see that the principle of harvest extends to how we manage the resources that God has given us.

This reminds us that we are called to be good stewards of everything God has entrusted us. If we are faithful with our little, God will trust us with more.

In summary, the principle of harvest teaches us that we will reap what we sow and how we sow. Furthermore, it outlines the understanding that the seeds we sow will leave our hands and enter our future to await our arrival.

Finally, we must realize that actions have consequences and we are called to be faithful stewards of all God has given us. As we reflect on this principle, may we be encouraged to give generously, to sow to please the Spirit, and to trust in God's promise that we will reap a harvest if we do not give up.

DAY 15 - THE PRINCIPLE OF HARVEST

2 Corinthians 9.6 *But this I say: He who sows sparingly will also reap sparingly, and he who sows bountifully will also reap bountifully.*

If I could give everyone a piece of advice, it would be — "Don't waste your life." God has given you more than you'll ever need. Most of the time, whenever giving is mentioned, our first thoughts are toward finances. While giving can include money, it is not always about money. When we fail to give of ourselves, we are wasting our lives. I've said this countless times in my circle, "The greatest gift you can give is the gift of yourself."

Here is an outline of Paul's giving strategy:

1. Be generous in giving:

The Word generous has the connotation of being "noble-born." Now that's powerful. When I am generous, I'm expressing my Nobility and Royalty. If this is the case, then what does it mean if I refuse to give?

Giving generously requires us to be selfless. Not putting our needs ahead of others. When we give generously, we demonstrate our trust in God's willingness and provision to bless others.

The most remarkable example is in the life of Jesus. He gave His life so that we can have a thriving life. He is the ultimate example of selflessness and generosity. His life serves as a model for us to follow.

2. Be willing to give:

Giving willingly involves being willing to share what we have with others. And it requires us to have a proper perspective on our possessions. We need to recognize that everything we have comes from God, and we are stewards of those resources. This means we should be willing to use what we have to help others and advance God's kingdom.

The widow in Mark 12 is an excellent example of giving willingly. Even though it was only two tiny coins, she donated everything. As a result, Jesus praised her for her generosity.

She had given more than all the others who had given out of their abundance. As a result, she was commended by Jesus for her gift.

3. Be cheerful in giving:
Giving cheerfully isn't about the act of giving itself. It's about our attitude toward giving. It is about having a joyful heart. One that finds joy in being a blessing to others. To give this way shows our trust in God's provision.

It requires us to have a proper perspective on our possessions. We need to recognize that everything we have comes from God, and we are stewards of His resources.

An example of giving cheerfully is the Macedonian churches (see 2 Corinthians 8:1-5). The Macedonians were going through a tough time. Despite severe trials and extreme poverty, they gave generously and joyfully.

As we strive to follow these concepts of giving, let's remember that our giving is not about meeting the needs of others. But it's about expressing our love for God and advancing His kingdom on earth.

DECLARATION
I will sow bountifully and reap bountifully. I believe that my giving will be joyful and abundant and that God will bless me for my generosity.

DAY 16 - THE PRINCIPLE OF HARVEST

Psalm 85:12 *The Lord will indeed give what is good, and our land will yield its harvest.*

Sowing requires labor, but harvest requires patience.

In agriculture, a harvest is the culmination of hard work and cultivation. We plant seeds, tend to the crops, and wait for the day when we can gather the harvest. We work now to reap later.

Let's look at a few aspects of harvest:

Harvest symbolizes a promise of God's faithfulness. Galatians 6 says, "Whatever you sow, that shall you reap." This promise of God is the sowing and reaping process.

Harvest is a natural part of life. There's nothing we can do without encountering the process of sowing and reaping. You go to the grocery, and you return with food. You go to church, and you return full of faith and hope. You go out to the mailbox, and you return with your mail.

Harvest is a process of time. After we sow our seeds, we must be persistent and patient in faith. Knowing that God will bring about our harvest in His time!

We are to harvest with Joy. While harvest requires patience, it's to be done with Joy. The Bible says that those who sow in tears will reap in joy.

So let us be encouraged and continue to sow the seeds God has given us. May the Lord grant us a bountiful harvest - not only in our fields but in our hearts and the lives of those around us.

DECLARATION
I declare that I will not be weary in doing good, for at the proper time, I will reap a harvest if I do not give up.

DAY 17 - THE PRINCIPLE OF HARVEST

Luke 6:38 *Give, and it will be given to you: good measure, pressed down, shaken together, and running over will be put into your bosom. For with the same measure that you use, it will be measured back to you."*

The concept of harvest is prevalent throughout the Bible. It symbolizes abundance, provision, and blessings. In a natural sense, harvest refers to gathering crops and fruits that have been sown and tended to over time. But spiritually, it can also represent God's blessings in our lives.

Reflecting on Luke 6:38 reminds us of the significance of sowing and reaping in our lives. This verse serves as a guiding principle for us. It promises blessings for our generosity.

It is easy to become fixated on our own needs and wants. But, we achieve true fulfillment through giving to others. Through this act, we can spread joy and impact the lives of those around us. In doing so, we allow ourselves to open up to receiving blessings that come in many shapes and sizes.

This is harvest—fruit for both ourselves and those around us. When we give, we are sowing seeds. And this seed, over time, will grow into a flourishing tree of generosity that bears fruit.

The harvest that follows our season of sowing will always bring about blessings. The seed is never wasted.   It has the potential to grow and bloom in ways we never imagined.

Let us then embrace the process of sowing and patiently await our harvest. As we do, let us also give generously and abundantly, for the measure we use to give will be the measure we receive in return.

DECLARATION
I declare that I will give with a willing and generous heart because God loves those who give freely.

DAY 18 - THE PRINCIPLE OF HARVEST

Proverbs 3:9-10 *Honor the Lord with your wealth and with the firstfruits of all your produce; then your barns will be filled with plenty, and your vats will be bursting with wine.*

Here we see two connected ideas, honor, and harvest. Although they don't seem to go together, they are essential to our relationship with God.

As believers, we are not to honor God out of obligation or to seek His favor. Instead, it's our way of acknowledging Him with respect and gratitude.

When we honor God, we acknowledge that all we have comes from Him. He is our source. We show gratitude and dependence when we recognize this. This act of honor pleases God and sets us on a path of abundance and prosperity. As we've read, when we honor God with our wealth, our barns will be filled with plenty, and our vats will burst with wine.

But honoring God isn't only about giving Him our material possessions. It is also about giving Him our hearts, lips, and lives. We honor God with our hearts when we put Him first and seek to please Him in all we do. We honor Him with our lips when we speak words of praise and thanksgiving. We honor Him with our lives when we live according to His will and strive to reflect His love and grace.

It is not always simple to honor God in these ways, but I can attest that it is always worthwhile. So, let's honor God. Let's give Him our wealth, hearts, lips, and lives.

DECLARATION
I am a giver and not a taker.

DAY 19 - THE PRINCIPLE OF HARVEST

Deuteronomy 11:13-15 - *13 So if you faithfully obey the commands I am giving you today—to love the Lord your God and to serve him with all your heart and with all your soul— **14** then I will send rain on your land in its season, both autumn and spring rains, so that you may gather in your grain, new wine and olive oil. **15** I will provide grass in the fields for your cattle, and you will eat and be satisfied.*

Deuteronomy 11:13 says, "Love the Lord your God and serve him with all your heart and all your soul." Our love should not be performed in a half-hearted manner but rather with total devotion. As we devote ourselves, we'll experience an abundance of rain for our crops and food for our livestock. Our fields will be lush and abundant, and our spirits will be fulfilled.

Disobedience, however, will result in lack and famine. Our harvests will be limited. Our spirits will thirst for the satisfaction that can only be found in obedience to God's Word.

It is easy to become complacent in our faith, to let our love and obedience to God wane. But we are called to renew our commitment to God, to hold fast to His Word, and obey His commands. Walking in obedience to God's Word leads to a closer relationship with Him. It gives us what we need to walk in His will and have peace that surpasses all understanding.

We have faith that our Heavenly Father guides us along the path of righteousness. Let us not be like the Israelites, who rejected God and endured forty years of suffering. Instead, we should adhere to the promise of blessings associated with obedience.

Let us renew our commitment to God as we reflect upon Deuteronomy 11:13-15. Let us love Him with all our heart and spirit and serve Him with gladness and submission.

May the rain of His blessings pour upon us as we walk in His ways. May our hearts be filled with the satisfaction that can only come from living a life devoted to our Creator.

DECLARATION
I declare my faithful obedience and love for God with all my heart and soul. He will bless me with rain for my crops and provide for my cattle, and I will eat and be satisfied.

DAY 20 - THE PRINCIPLE OF HARVEST

WEEKLY DECLARATIONS

Take this time to make the declarations we've made throughout the week.

I declare that I will sow bountifully and reap bountifully. I believe that my giving will be joyful and abundant and that God will bless me for my generosity.

I declare that I will not be weary in doing good, for at the proper time, I will reap a harvest if I do not give up.

I declare I will give with a willing and generous heart, for I believe God loves those who give freely.

I am a giver and not a taker.

I declare my faithful obedience and love for God with all my heart and soul. He will bless me with rain for my crops and provide for my cattle, and I will eat and be satisfied.

DAY 21 - THE PRINCIPLE OF HARVEST

ACTIVATION

Jeremiah 30:2 *Thus speaks the Lord God of Israel, saying: 'Write in a book for yourself all the words that I have spoken to you.*

Take some time to write what God has spoken to you this week. What areas do you need to change, and what steps will you take to make those changes?

_____

_____

_____

_____

_____

_____

_____

_____

_____

_____

_____

_____

THE DREAMER'S ANTHEM

Potential is not what you have done,
But what you are yet to do,
There are dreams that are still to be spun,
Your horizons are waiting for you.

For every day is a new chance,
To embrace the future ahead,
And with each step, you can enhance,
The path that you have been led.

The past may hold some regrets,
And mistakes that you wish to forget,
But it's never too late to reset,
And seek the dreams that you have not met.

For potential is a seed that's sown,
A promise waiting to be grown,
And with each day that passes by,
The fruit of your potential can multiply.

So don't let the past hold you down,
Or the doubts that may spin you around,
For your potential is waiting to be found,
In the dreams that you have not yet crowned.

Embrace the future with open hands,
And trust the journey, where it lands,
For potential is not what you've done,
But what you are yet to become.

- Lane Hawkins

4. THE PRINCIPLE OF POTENTIAL

What you have done is no longer your potential. Potential is what you can do but have not yet done. - **Dr. Myles Munroe**

Allow me to make a few statements here:

- Potential is the power of my life, and purpose is the reason for my life.
- Potential is the how, but purpose is the why. Potential reveals purpose, and purpose answers potential.
- No one is as blind as someone who cannot see their potential.

Allow me to explain.   The energy that drives me forward is my potential, while purpose provides meaning to my life.

Potential is about "how" I exist, while purpose is the profound "why" I exist.   As I discover my potential it reveals my purpose, and my purpose strengthens and expands my potential.   These two elements work together in a synergistic relationship.

The driving force behind my life is my potential, while my purpose provides the reason for living. Potential show us how to achieve our goals, while purpose gives us a reason to strive for them. These two concepts are intertwined with potential revealing purpose and purpose answering potential. Those who cannot see their potential are truly blind to their abilities.

Allow me to make a few statements here:

- Potential is the power of my life, and purpose is the reason for my life.
- Potential is the "how," but purpose is the "why."
- Potential reveals purpose, and purpose answers potential.

Allow me to explain. The energy that drives me forward is my potential, while my purpose provides meaning to my life. Potential is about "how" I exist, while purpose is the profound "why." As I discover my potential, it reveals my purpose, and my purpose strengthens and expands my potential. These two elements work together in a synergistic relationship.

The driving force behind my life is my potential. Purpose provides the reason for living, but it's potential that empowers my life. Potential shows us how to achieve our goals, while purpose gives us a reason to strive for them. These two concepts are intertwined with potential, revealing purpose and purpose answering potential.

Those who cannot see their potential are truly blind to their abilities.

Dale Carnegie wrote the book titled "How to Win Friends and Influence People." It was an overnight success selling over 15 million copies. Mr. Carnegie was a master at identifying people with great potential. He was once asked by a news reporter how he had managed to hire 43 men who were all millionaires. He said well, it's simple; none of them were millionaires when I hired them. All of them became millionaires while they were working for me. They wanted to know how he knew they had the potential to become wealthy. He said you find potential the same way you find gold. Several tons of dirt must be moved to get one ounce of gold.

> *No one is as blind as a person who cannot see their potential.*

But you don't go into the mine looking for dirt; you go in looking for gold. You look for potential.

Everything in life has the potential to be great. Everyone has potential, and everyone is born with it. Potential is God-given. What we do with our God-given potential is what will define our lives. It is sad to see so many people live far beneath their level of potential.

A term we use for God is Omnipotent. We believe Him to be "All-powerful," and we know this to be true. God is all-powerful. Within the Word, omnipotent is the word potent. This is the root of the word potential. To say that one possesses potential is to say that one has power.

Although the word "potential" doesn't appear in the Bible, there is a word that comes very close; it's the Word possible. According to Vines Dictionary, the Greek Word *dynatos* means: able, powerful, mighty, and strong, and the Word possible is a derivative.

For many, potential is analogous to a seed. It's been said that within the seed is a mighty forest. But the forest will only become if the seed reaches its potential. Its possibility is a hidden ability that must be developed.

Maximizing our God-given potential is essential for thriving in life. According to the Bible, God endowed us with unique talents, abilities, and potential. Our potential is a gift from God, and our responsibility is to develop and maximize it.

Thrive: Igniting Your Fire for a Fulfilled Life

To realize our full potential, we must first recognize its purpose of serving God and others, not ourselves. We must have a humble heart, depend on God, and acknowledge our need for His guidance and strength (Proverbs 3:5-6). We must also be willing to take risks and step out in faith, believing that God will equip and empower us to do the work He has assigned us (Philippians 4:13).

Personal fulfillment, happiness, and a sense of purpose are all benefits of reaching our full potential. Living up to our full potential gives us confidence, creativity, and innovation. It creates a positive transformational ripple effect. It enables us to make significant societal contributions, effect positive change, leave a lasting legacy, and inspire others to do the same.

Furthermore, when we develop and use our potential for the glory of God, we experience spiritual growth and personal transformation. We become more like Christ, who used His gifts and talents to serve others and carry out God's plan (Philippians 2:5-8). We also strengthen our relationship with God, who rejoices when His children use their abilities to bring Him honor and praise.

DAY 22 - THE PRINCIPLE OF POTENTIAL

Genesis 37:5-6 *Joseph had a dream, and when he told it to his brothers, they hated him all the more. 6 He said to them, "Listen to this dream I had: 7 We were binding sheaves of grain out in the field when suddenly my sheaf rose and stood upright, while your sheaves gathered around mine and bowed down to it.*

What do you dream about? What has God been speaking to you? These dreams are important. Your dreams are a revelation of your potential. It's a revelation of God's unique plans for you! But if you're not connected to him, you lose out on everything he wants to do in your life.

Joseph was a young man with immense potential. He was the youngest of twelve brothers and was his father's favorite. His brothers, jealous of the attention he was getting, plotted against him. Wanting to kill him, instead, they sold him into slavery. Joseph's story is a testament to the power of potential.

Potential is the dormant power that lies within each of us. Joseph had potential. He was a dreamer, and his dreams reflected his greatness. His dreams revealed that one day he would be a leader with power and influence over his family and even the entire region.

Like Joseph, each of us has the capacity for greatness. We have the potential to achieve our dreams and to impact those around us in order to make a positive impact and a difference in the world.

But, potential left in this state is not enough. It's not enough to say that we have potential. Potential unrealized will help no one. We must work hard to develop and refine our skills, gain knowledge and experience, and become the best version of ourselves.

Joseph's story reminds us that those around us can sometimes threaten our potential. Others may become jealous of our abilities. They may seek to tear us down to build themselves up. We must remain steadfast in pursuing greatness, not allowing others to dim our light or hold us back.

Joseph's story points to the fact that potential is God-given. It is a gift that we are called to steward and develop, using it to honor and glorify Him. Our ultimate purpose is not to chase after our ambition or success. But to use our potential to serve others and make a positive impact on the world around us.

The story of Joseph reveals the power of potential. Our potential is a gift, one that we must treasure and develop, using it to honor God and help those around us. We can achieve greatness, but it requires hard work, dedication, and a steadfast commitment to our dreams. As we navigate life's challenges and obstacles, we must hold on to our faith, trusting in God's plan and purpose.

DECLARATION
I am confident in God's plan and purpose for my life.

DAY 23 - THE PRINCIPLE OF POTENTIAL

Jeremiah 29:11 *For I know the thoughts that I think toward you, says the Lord, thoughts of peace and not of evil, to give you a future and a hope.*

God has a plan for us.

This is a powerful message. It brings hope to believers worldwide, reminding us that our lives are not left to chance. But it's authored and designed by a loving God who has our best interest in mind.

Some may find it hard to understand the idea of "potential." Not sure if we're living up to it. But potential isn't something we need to "live up to," but more so, something we're to release. Are we making the most of the gifts God has given us? Or are we doing what God wants us to do? Potential is more of a question than a reality. But Jeremiah 29:11 tells us that God has a plan and a purpose for our lives and wants us to do well.

We can have faith and hope when we think about what God has put in our lives. Knowing that our God is the same yesterday, today, and forever and that He can do anything. He isn't limited by how weak we are. Instead, He works through us, giving us the power to do great things for His praise.

The thing is, we are often our own worst enemy when it comes to understanding and appreciating our potential. We are plagued with self-doubt, fear, and insecurity that can paralyze us and prevent us from living our best lives. But we must remember that our identity is not in ourselves or what we do. It is in Christ who lives within us.

As the scripture says, "We can do all things through Christ who strengthens us." therefore, we have power, hope, and the potential to do what he's called us to do. His plan, purpose, and destiny for us are all working toward our good. But it's up to us to allow Him to work in and through us, empowering us to live up to our potential.

Thrive: Igniting Your Fire for a Fulfilled Life

Potential lies within each of us, waiting to be unleashed by the power of God. May we all be empowered to live lives of purpose and passion, achieving great things for God's kingdom.

DECLARATION
In every season of my life, I choose to align my will with the will of God. I surrender my desires and aspirations to His divine purpose, knowing His plans are far greater than mine.

DAY 24 - THE PRINCIPLE OF POTENTIAL

Colossians 3:22-24 - 23 *And whatever you do, do it heartily, as to the Lord and not to men, 24 knowing that from the Lord you will receive the reward of the inheritance; for[a] you serve the Lord Christ.*

When we are living out our potential, it's not only about doing a good job. It's about doing it to the best of our abilities and with a heart of service.

I used to work for a Fortune 500 company. Early in my career, I found myself in some trouble. I'd gotten accustomed to taking shortcuts, and my work product suffered greatly. To turn things around, I was placed on a 6-month probationary period. I was recently married some months earlier, and we had just found out my wife was pregnant. I was miserable.

After I signed the memo, I went to my car for a break. I began to cry (I'm a big crybaby) and complain (I mean pray) to God about how unfair this was. I pointed fingers at everyone except me. During this episode, God spoke very clearly to me. He asked a simple question. "Who do you work for?" In a whimpering voice, I named the company. "Nooo, who do you work for?" Because of the need for more understanding, we went back and forth a few times.

When I finally understood the question, "Who do you work for?" My reply was quick. "You, God, I work for you!" Then came the kicker. "Then act like it!"

This moment has become a life principle for me. Everything I do, I work for the Lord. This aids me in releasing my potential.

In our daily lives, it is easy to become complacent. Going through the motions with little thought or effort. We may feel that our work is insignificant or that our efforts go unnoticed. Our lives can take on a whole new level of importance and meaning when we view our work as an opportunity to fulfill our potential and glorify God.

When we put our best foot forward and work towards our potential, we can inspire and impact others around us. Our dedication and passion can motivate others to strive toward their potential, and together, we can create a ripple effect of positive change.

But reaching our potential requires us to overcome obstacles and setbacks. Keeping our eyes fixed on the ultimate goal.

So let us strive towards our potential in all we do, whether in our work, relationships, or personal growth. Let's seek to honor God in every aspect of our lives and trust in his plan to lead us toward a life of purpose and fulfillment.

May we never settle for mediocrity.   We have the potential to achieve greatness.

DECLARATION
I am successful in all my endeavors.

DAY 25 - THE PRINCIPLE OF POTENTIAL

Acts 1.8 *But you shall receive power when the Holy Spirit has come upon you, and you shall be witnesses to Me in Jerusalem, and in all Judea and Samaria, and to the end of the earth.*

POWER! UNLIMITED POWER!

In the revealing scene from *Star Wars: Episode III - Revenge of the Sith*, the Sith Lord Darth Sidious declares his ultimate desire, stating, "Power! Unlimited power!"

Acts 1:8 is a similar pronouncement. This verse is rich with potential and promise. It speaks of a power that comes only from the Holy Spirit and a witness that reaches the ends of the earth.

As believers, we have access to this same power and potential. We are called to be witnesses of the gospel to all nations. But sometimes, there may be a feeling of being inadequate for the task at hand. We may question our abilities and wonder if we have what it takes to fulfill such a daunting calling.

In these moments, we must remember that our potential isn't about what we have.   But, it comes from the Holy Spirit within us. The same power that raised Jesus from the dead is available to us. We need only surrender ourselves to Him and allow His ability to work through us.

So, let's not be discouraged by perceived limitations. Instead, let's embrace the potential that comes from the Holy Spirit. Let's rely on His power to be witnesses of the gospel to all nations. So walk boldly in that power, trusting that He who called us is faithful to complete the work He began in us.

DECLARATION
The Holy Spirit empowers me to live a life of victory and triumph.

DAY 26 - THE PRINCIPLE OF POTENTIAL

1 Corinthians 9.24 *Do you not know that those who run in a race all run, but one receives the prize? Run in such a way that you may obtain it.*

We come across a profound concept that speaks to our innermost being - the idea of being a winner.

The city of Corinth would host the Isthmian Games every two to three years. An event that was second only to the Olympic Games. The Corinthians were great sports lovers and proud of this tremendous athletic festival.

Paul uses this analogy of the games to encourage his Christian brothers and sisters that they would have a zealous faith in Jesus Christ.

We're encouraged to run in such a way as to obtain the prize. It reminds us that we should strive to be the best version of ourselves in every aspect of life. We shouldn't be satisfied with being average or comfortable. Instead, we should push ourselves to reach new levels of success.

Being a winner doesn't only pertain to natural success, such as winning a race. No, it encompasses all areas of life and character - as a spouse, parent, friend, colleague, or individual. Every decision we make, and every action we take, is to be inspired by our desire to excel. To be the best we can be.

To stand atop the podium of life will demand discipline, determination, and perseverance. We'll have to set goals, make plans, and take action. We cannot sit back and wait for things to happen. Be bold and courageous. Take the initiative. Be proactive.

Ultimately, our prize is not only earthly rewards or recognition. They're eternal rewards. Reward that comes from knowing that we have lived our lives to the fullest. We have made a positive impact on others, and we have honored God with our actions.

So allow me to ask you a question. How are you running? I hope you replied that you are "Running to win?"

DECLARATION
I am a winner and not a loser.

DAY 27 - THE PRINCIPLE OF POTENTIAL
WEEKLY DECLARATIONS

Take this time to make the declarations we've made throughout the week.

I am confident in God's plan and purpose for my life.

In every season of my life, I choose to align my will with the will of God. I surrender my desires and aspirations to His divine purpose, knowing His plans are far greater than mine.

I am successful in all my endeavors.

The Holy Spirit empowers me to live a life of victory and triumph.

I am a winner and not a loser.

DAY 28 - THE PRINCIPLE OF POTENTIAL

ACTIVATION

Jeremiah 30:2 *Thus speaks the Lord God of Israel, saying: 'Write in a book for yourself all the words that I have spoken to you.*

Take some time to write what God has spoken to you this week. What areas do you need to change, and what steps will you take to make those changes?

INVINCIBLE

Be strong and of good courage, do not fear,
For the Lord your God is with you, always near,
In every step, He walks beside,
A constant presence, a faithful guide.

Though troubles come and doubts arise,
His love and power will make us rise,
For with Him, we can face anything,
And in His strength, we find the power to sing.

Do not be afraid, nor be dismayed,
For in His love, all fears do fade,
For the Lord your God is with you, wherever you go,
A beacon of hope, a source of light aglow.

So walk with confidence, head held high,
With every step, draw near to the Most High,
For He is with you, His love surrounds,
A rock to stand on, a firm foundation found.

Be strong and of good courage, do not fear,
For the Lord your God is always near,
In His love, we find the strength to stand,
And in His presence, we know where we stand.

- Lane Hawkins

5. THE PRINCIPLE OF ENDURANCE

Hebrews 10:36 *For you have need of endurance, so that after you have done the will of God, you may receive the promise:*

"Endurance is not just the ability to bear a hard thing, but to turn it into glory." Endurance is His power to go on despite difficulties, not merely surviving. It is not accomplished with a "Whew, I made it" mentality. It is the ability to persevere in the face of adversity, hardship, and challenge with faith and unwavering trust in God. It is essential to a Christian's faith.

> *"Endurance is not just the ability to bear a hard thing, but to turn it into glory."*
> *- Philip Yancy.*

We're encouraged to persevere in our faith and do what is right, even when it is complex or challenging. Let's explore how endurance can help us to thrive in our lives and achieve the goals that we set for ourselves.

One way that endurance helps us to thrive is by building resilience. We become more resilient when we face challenges and overcome them through our endurance. Every time we go through something, we are better able to handle stress and adversity in the future, and we are less likely to be discouraged by setbacks. Resilience is a critical ingredient in success, and endurance is one of the most effective ways to build it.

Another way that endurance helps us to thrive is by increasing our self-confidence. When we set goals for ourselves and work tirelessly to achieve them, we develop confidence in our abilities. As we gain more and more through our endurance, our faith grows, and we become more successful in all areas of our lives. We begin to see ourselves as capable, and this belief in ourselves can be a powerful motivator.

> *When life is just too tough, God's faithfulness is tougher. Even if you're tempted to quit, you can make it through.* **- Ed Cole**

Finally, endurance helps us to thrive by giving us a sense of purpose. When we have a goal that we are working towards and are willing to do whatever it takes to achieve it, we feel a sense of purpose. A sense of meaning and significance drives us, which can be a powerful motivator. And when we have a sense of purpose, we are more likely to be happy and fulfilled and less likely to be distracted by the trivialities of life.

Examples of endurance are throughout the Bible, from Noah's perseverance through the flood to Job's steadfastness in the face of great suffering. Jesus' life is perhaps the most famous example of endurance. On the cross, Jesus endured great suffering while remaining steadfast in his faith in God, even in death.

Thrive: Igniting Your Fire for a Fulfilled Life

In his letters to the early Christian churches, the Apostle Paul also wrote extensively about endurance. In his letter to the Romans, Paul encouraged believers to endure suffering, saying, "We also boast in our sufferings, knowing that suffering produces endurance, and endurance produces character, and character produces hope" (Romans 5:3-4).

In conclusion, Hebrews 10:36 reminds us of the importance of endurance in our lives, which can build resilience, increase self-confidence, and find purpose by developing this quality. When we endure in the face of adversity, we can thrive and achieve the goals we set for ourselves. It is not always easy, but it is always worth it.

DAY 29 - THE PRINCIPLE OF ENDURANCE

Philippians 4:6-7 - *6 Be anxious for nothing, but in everything by prayer and supplication, with thanksgiving, let your requests be made known to God; 7 and the peace of God, which surpasses all understanding, will guard your hearts and minds through Christ Jesus.*

Have you ever felt anxious? Anxiety or worry, if left unaddressed, is a strong force that can break people down. Both will leave us frustrated, baffled, and confused. As God tells us, the remedy is to pray, bringing every concern and care to Him.

It is easy to grow overwhelmed during difficult and stressful times. The stresses of daily life can put a strain on our minds. It will make us doubt ourselves and our ability to persevere.

The passage begins with a powerful directive: "Do not be anxious..." In a constantly changing world, it can be tempting to worry about the future, but the verse offers a solution. Instead of worrying, we have to bring our concerns to God.

How often do we try to shoulder our burdens alone? Forgetting that we have a loving and powerful Father who is eager to help us? Instead, we can pray about any and everything—nothing is too big or too small for God.

But it doesn't stop there. We are also encouraged to approach God with an attitude of thanksgiving, recognizing all the ways in which He has already blessed us. When we focus on gratitude instead of fear, it is easier to trust God. He will provide for us and carry us through the darkest of times.

And what is the result of this trust? "the peace of God, which surpasses all understanding, will guard your hearts and minds in Christ Jesus." When we surrender our anxiety and worry to God, His peace fills us. We can, then, endure with a strength that defies explanation.

Endurance doesn't always mean running a marathon or climbing a mountain. Sometimes it means putting one foot in front of the other, trusting that God will sustain us. When we meditate on Philippians 4:6-7 and seek to apply the truth in this passage to our lives, we will find a source of endurance that will carry us through even the darkest valleys.

DECLARATION
I am protected from fear, anxiety, and worry.

DAY 30 - THE PRINCIPLE OF ENDURANCE

Joshua 1:9 *Have I not commanded you? Be strong and of good courage; do not be afraid, nor be dismayed, for the Lord your God is with you wherever you go.*

God's words to Joshua remain relevant to us today.

Have you ever felt afraid of stepping out of your comfort zone? Did you feel anxious or uncertain about it? From my own experience, I know how daunting it can be to face the unknown. But I also know how it feels to be brave enough to go where you've never been.

As children of God, we are to live a life of courage. I know that's a bold statement, but God has given us a spirit of power, love, and a sound mind (2 Timothy 1:7). With Him, nothing is impossible (Mark 10:27). He commands us to be strong and not to be afraid, no matter how big or small the task. Whether starting a new job, moving to a new city, or even sharing the gospel with a friend. Be courageous and trust in the Lord with all our hearts (Proverbs 3:5-6).

There may be times when you experience fear, doubt, or uncertainty, but you can choose to push past those feelings and trust the Lord. We must know that He is faithful and will never leave us nor forsake us. Courage enables our willingness to step away from our safety nets and into the unknown. We rest on the promise that God has a purpose and a plan for our lives.

Be strong and remind yourself daily that you are also to be courageous. You have been given a spirit of power and love and a sound mind, and God is with you wherever you go. Don't allow fear to hold you back from experiencing all God has for you. Instead, trust in Him, and He will guide you on the path of righteousness (Psalm 23:3).

Remember that courage is not the absence of fear but the willingness to trust the Lord despite our fears. So go forth, be strong and courageous, and let God's love and power propel you to greater heights. May this devotion inspire you to overcome your fears, take risks, and pursue the life God has called you to.

DECLARATION
I will not be discouraged, for the Lord, my God, will be with me wherever I go.

DAY 31 - THE PRINCIPLE OF ENDURANCE

Romans 8:33 *Who shall bring a charge against God's elect? It is God who justifies.* **34** *Who is he who condemns? It is Christ who died, and furthermore is also risen, who is even at the right hand of God, who also makes intercession for us.* **35** *Who shall separate us from the love of Christ? Shall tribulation, or distress, or persecution, or famine, or nakedness, or peril, or sword?* **36** *As it is written: "For Your sake we are killed all day long; We are accounted as sheep for the slaughter."* **37** *Yet in all these things we are more than conquerors through Him who loved us.* **38** *For I am persuaded that neither death nor life, nor angels nor principalities nor powers, nor things present nor things to come,* **39** *nor height nor depth, nor any other created thing, shall be able to separate us from the love of God which is in Christ Jesus our Lord.*

A conqueror is someone who gains a decisive victory in battle.

Here Paul answers the question of what can separate us from the love of God. He emphatically answers it with a sturdy "Nothing;" nothing can separate us from the love of God.

When Paul writes, "Yet in all these things," he refers to the difficulties and trials we may face. These hardships can range from health, finances, family, and more. Yet, despite these trials, we are given the chance to become "more than conquerors." This means we can overcome these hardships through our faith in Jesus Christ.

We do not conquer these obstacles in our strength but through Him who loved us. When we focus on His love, we become stronger, more resilient, and more determined. We can be steadfast in our faith, even when it feels as if the world is crashing around us. We are filled with peace and reassurance by placing our trust in Him. We must know He is with us even in the darkest moments.

Reflecting on this verse, let's remember the significance of Christ's sacrifice. His unwavering love for us poured out through His death for our sins. He has provided an opportunity for us to live lives of abundance in the face of our struggles. We can find victory in Jesus Christ even in our most challenging circumstances. We can be assured that He has already won all our battles and that we are more than conquerors through Him.

DECLARATION
I will not quit, for I am a conqueror through Christ who loves me.

DAY 32 - THE PRINCIPLE OF ENDURANCE

Deuteronomy 31. 8 *Do not be afraid or discouraged, for the Lord will personally go ahead of you. He will be with you; he will neither fail you nor abandon you.*

In the midst of life's challenges and uncertainties, it is natural for fear and discouragement to try to creep into our hearts. We may question our abilities, doubt our strength, and wonder if we have what it takes to overcome the obstacle(s) ahead.

These powerful words from God remind us that we are not alone in our journey. We have a faithful companion who goes before us, preparing the way and paving a path of victory. In His infinite wisdom and love, the Lord assures us that He will never leave our side. He promises to personally accompany us through every trial, every challenge, and every season of life.

It is in the presence of God that we find the strength to endure. When we realize that the Creator of the universe walks beside us, fear loses its grip, and discouragement dissipates. Our focus shifts from our limitations to the boundless power of our Heavenly Father. We begin to understand that our ability to endure depends not on our strength alone but on the limitless strength of God that dwells within us.

As we face trials and hardships, let us remember that God's presence is not just a comforting idea but a tangible reality. His Spirit resides within us, guiding, strengthening, and upholding us. We can draw from His unending well of grace, courage, and wisdom. We can tap into His unwavering faithfulness and trust in His perfect plan for our lives.

DECLARATION
I declare that I will not be afraid or discouraged, for the Lord personally goes ahead of me. He is with me; He will never fail me nor abandon me.

DAY 33 - THE PRINCIPLE OF ENDURANCE

Isaiah 41:10 *Fear not, for I am with you; Be not dismayed, for I am your God. I will strengthen you, Yes, I will help you; I will uphold you with My righteous right hand.'*

In Isaiah 41:10, God says, "Fear not, for I am with you; be not dismayed, for I am your God; I will strengthen you, I will help you, I will uphold you with my righteous right hand." This verse is a source of great comfort and peace for many Christians, as it reminds us that we do not need to be afraid or anxious, for God is always with us.

When we feel overwhelmed by life's challenges, the words of Isaiah 41:10 can offer us hope and assurance. We can take comfort in knowing that we have a God bigger than any problem or obstacle we may face. He is our protector, our guide, and our source of strength.

Sometimes, it may feel like we are all alone in our struggles, but Isaiah 41:10 reminds us that we are never truly alone. God is with us and will never leave or forsake us. Even in our darkest moments, we can find hope and peace in His presence which will keep us from fainting and losing heart.

The scripture affirms that God is sovereign and in control. We can trust in Him to work all things together for our good and His glory. He will uphold us with His righteous right hand and lead us through every trial and tribulation.

As we meditate on this powerful verse, let us take comfort in knowing that God is with us always. Let us trust in His promises and find rest in His presence. For in Him, we have all we need to face life's challenges and emerge victorious.

DECLARATION
I will not lose heart, for the Lord is the strength of my life.

DAY 34 - THE PRINCIPLE OF ENDURANCE
WEEKLY DECLARATIONS

Take this time to make the declarations we've made throughout the week.

I am protected from fear, anxiety, and worry.

I will not be discouraged, for the Lord, my God, will be with me wherever I go.

I will not quit, for I am a conqueror through Christ who loves me.

I declare that I will not be afraid or discouraged, for the Lord personally goes ahead of me. He is with me; He will never fail me nor abandon me.

I will not lose heart, for the Lord is the strength of my life.

DAY 35 - THE PRINCIPLE OF ENDURANCE

ACTIVATION

Jeremiah 30:2 *Thus speaks the Lord God of Israel, saying: 'Write in a book for yourself all the words I have spoken to you.*

Take some time to write what God has spoken to you this week. What areas do you need to change, and what steps will you take to make those changes?

THE WARRIORS CREED

When darkness descends like a shroud,
We rise up, strong and unbowed,
For within us, a light shines bright,
Guiding us through the darkest night.

For in the face of every adversity,
We find the power to rise above - no infirmity,
With courage and conviction, we forge ahead,
And leave our fears and doubts behind for dead.

For every crisis is an opportunity,
To rise and meet the challenge with no ambiguity,
To face our fears and embrace the unknown,
And show the world what we're made of, and that is stone.

To be unmovable and unshakable in times of trial
Our faith is strong- there's no denial
In the hottest of trial, we find our strength,
We emerge, victorious, at any length,

So let us embrace each challenge we face,
With strength, courage, and grace,
For we are warriors, fierce and bold,
And in our hearts, victory shall unfold.

- Lane Hawkins

6. THE PRINCIPLE OF OVERCOMING CRISIS

Genesis 50:20 As for you, you meant evil against me, but God meant it for good, to bring it about that many people should be kept alive, as they are today.

A crisis can be defined as a situation in your life over which you have no control. Every individual will face some form of crisis in their life. And yet, what is considered a crisis for one may not be for another. It will depend on the control one has in or over his/her situation.

No particular situation can be considered a crisis for everyone, but everyone will endure turmoil. God does not consider anything a crisis because He has absolute control over every situation.

Joseph's story is one of the most potent examples of how overcoming a crisis can lead to thriving. Despite being sold into slavery, falsely accused of a crime, and imprisoned for years, Joseph remained faithful to God and worked towards his goals. Eventually, he interpreted the Pharaoh's dreams and was appointed the second-in-command in Egypt.

A lesson in Joseph's story teaches us several essential things about the power of overcoming a crisis. First, it teaches us the importance of forgiveness. Joseph could have easily held a grudge against his brothers, but he forgave them.

> *"The ultimate measure of a man is not where he stands in the moments of comfort, but where he stands at times of challenge and controversy."*
> **- Martin Luther King**

Second, the story of Joseph teaches us the importance of perseverance. Despite facing countless obstacles and setbacks, Joseph never gave up. He continued to trust in God and work towards his goals, even when it seemed like all hope was lost. This perseverance ultimately led to his success and prosperity.

One of the most remarkable aspects of Joseph's story is his ability to find meaning in his struggles. Rather than becoming bitter or defeated, Joseph recognized that his difficult experiences were purposeful. He realized that his suffering had led him to hold a position where he could help others, and he experienced a sense of fulfillment in this role.

This is an essential lesson for us to learn as well. When we face crisis and adversity, it can be easy to become consumed by our pain and lose sight of the bigger picture. However, seeing how our struggles help us grow and help others, we can find a sense of purpose and meaning at all times, in every situation.

Ultimately, this is a powerful story of resilience and strength. Throughout his trials, Joseph never lost faith in God. In the face of incredible adversity, he overcame several crises and thrived. And like Joseph, if we apply the lessons of forgiveness and perseverance. If we trust in God and find meaning in our struggles, we can overcome our crises and find fulfillment and success amid our challenges.

DAY 36 - THE PRINCIPLE OF OVERCOMING CRISIS

Psalm 46.1 *God is our refuge and strength, A very present help in trouble.*

Life can be unpredictable and challenging, but the Lord is always there to protect and sustain us. He is a reliable source of strength and refuge when we feel overwhelmed or afraid. When we feel like we are in the midst of a storm, we can trust in God's steadfast love and faithfulness to carry us through.

As believers, we are called to be conquerors. We must face and overcome the challenges that come our way. We cannot do this alone, but with God as our refuge and strength, we can conquer all things through Him who strengthens us (Philippians 4:13).

Jesus said, "In this world, you will have trouble. But take heart! I have overcome the world" (John 16:33). We can be conquerors through Christ because He has already conquered the world.

When we face challenges, let us remember that God is our refuge and strength, and He is ready to help us. Let us lean on Him and trust Him to guide us through difficult times. As we do so, we can be confident that we will come out victorious through Him who loves us.

DECLARATION
I declare that God is my refuge and strength in times of trouble.

DAY 37 - THE PRINCIPLE OF OVERCOMING CRISIS

Philippians 4:6 *Be anxious for nothing, but in everything by prayer and supplication, with thanksgiving, let your requests be made known to God;*

When we face a crisis, feeling anxious and worried is natural. We might be afraid of the unknown, uncertain about the future, or overwhelmed by our circumstances. However, God's word reminds us that we don't have to face these challenges alone. Instead, we can pray to Him and ask for His help.

The key to overcoming crises is to trust in God's promises and to seek His guidance. In Philippians 4:6, we're instructed to present our requests to God with thanksgiving. So, we should approach Him with a heart of gratitude, acknowledging all the ways He has already blessed us and expressing our trust in His provision for the future.

Prayer is a powerful tool for overcoming crises because it allows us to connect with God and receive His peace. When we pray, we can lay our burdens at His feet and ask for His wisdom and guidance. We can also find comfort in knowing God listens and cares about our needs.

DECLARATION
I declare I will not be anxious, for God has promised to care for me.

DAY 38 - THE PRINCIPLE OF OVERCOMING CRISIS

Romans 8:28 *And we know that all things work together for good to those who love God, to those who are the called according to His purpose.*

This is a familiar verse to many believers, offering hope during trials and struggles.

We can confidently face any challenge or obstacle when we trust that all things are working together for our good. We can have peace knowing that God is in control, and we can press on with the assurance that everything is working out for our benefit.

As conquerors, we can see the world around us differently than others. We can see opportunities for growth and transformation in every situation, and we can approach challenges with the mindset of an overcomer. Instead of being overcome by the world, we can overcome it through the power of God and His plan for our lives.

Let us hold fast to the truth of Romans 8:28 and embrace our identity as conquerors in Christ. With this mindset, we can face every trial and difficulty with confidence and faith, knowing that God is with us and everything works together for our good.

DECLARATION
I declare that I am a child of God, and all things work together for my good.

DAY 39 - THE PRINCIPLE OF OVERCOMING CRISIS

Isaiah 45:24 *He shall say, 'Surely in the Lord, I have righteousness and strength. To Him, men shall come, And all shall be ashamed Who are incensed against Him.*

When facing challenges, we often think we must handle them alone, but this verse tells us that deliverance and strength come from the Lord alone. When we trust Him, we can access all the power we need to overcome any obstacle. With God, we can conquer anything that comes our way.

Being a conqueror doesn't mean that we won't face difficulties or hardships. It means that we have the strength and the faith to face them head-on, knowing that God is with us every step of the way.

Today, let us again remember that we are conquerors through Christ Jesus. With God, we can conquer anything. We can face anything that comes our way because we have the strength of God within us. Let us lean on Him for our deliverance and trust that He will guide us through every trial.

DECLARATION
I declare that I am clothed in God's strength and will not be defeated.

DAY 40 - THE PRINCIPLE OF OVERCOMING CRISIS

Psalm 18:2 *The Lord is my rock and my fortress and my deliverer; My God, my strength, in whom I will trust; My shield and the horn of my salvation, my stronghold.*

The Lord is my rock!

Life is filled with obstacles and trials that can leave us feeling overwhelmed and powerless. Yet, as followers of Christ, we have a powerful ally who empowers us to overcome every challenge that comes our way. In Psalm 18:2, the psalmist beautifully describes the Lord's multifaceted nature and how He equips us to triumph over adversity.

Just as a solid rock provides a firm foundation, God is an unshakable source of strength. When we face seemingly insurmountable difficulties, we can rely on His unwavering presence to give us stability and endurance. In Him, we find the courage to stand firm, knowing that He is the immovable foundation upon which we can anchor our lives.

Additionally, the Lord is our fortress and deliverer. In times of distress, He is our safe haven, our place of refuge and protection. When we feel trapped and overwhelmed by the trials of life, we can find comfort and security in the arms of our heavenly Father. He is the One who rescues us from the grip of despair, delivering us from the power of our enemies and the snares of temptation.

Finally, the psalmist declares that the Lord is our shield and stronghold. He is our defense against the attacks of the enemy. Just as a shield guards and deflects arrows, our God shields us from harm and preserves us in the face of adversity. He is our stronghold, a mighty fortress that surrounds us with His love and power. In Him, we find refuge and strength, enabling us to face every trial with confidence and victory.

Whatever challenge you may be facing today, take heart and remember the promises found in Psalm 18:2. Embrace the truth that the Lord is your rock, fortress, and deliverer. Trust in His unwavering strength and protection.

DECLARATION
I declare that God is my shield and source of protection in every situation.

DAY 40 - THE PRINCIPLE OF OVERCOMING CRISIS

ACTIVATION

Jeremiah 30:2 *Thus speaks the Lord God of Israel, saying: 'Write in a book for yourself all the words I have spoken to you.*

Take some time to write what God has spoken to you this week. What areas do you need to change, and what steps will you take to make those changes?

FINAL THOUGHTS

Congratulations on completing the 40-Day of Transformation devotional *"THRIVE: Igniting your Inner Fire for a Fulfilled Life."*

I hope this journey has been a meaningful and transformative experience for you and that you've gained valuable insights into God's desire for you to thrive.

Throughout the past 40 days, we explored essential principles such as Release, Harvest, Potential, Endurance, and Overcoming Crisis. These provide a foundation for us to live our lives with purpose and intentionality and navigate the challenges and opportunities that come our way.

As you apply these principles, I pray you will experience a more profound connection with God and see the fruit of your efforts in greater peace, joy, and fulfillment.

Remember, transformation is an ongoing process requiring consistent effort and commitment. But with God's help and the support of those around us, we can continue to grow and thrive and become the best version of ourselves that we were created to be.

May God bless you on your journey, and may you continue to seek His will and purpose for your life.

God's Best to you!

ABOUT THE AUTHOR

Pastor Lane hails from Lake Charles, Louisiana, and is deeply devoted to his faith as a man of God. His heart is filled with enthusiasm for the Almighty, His Word, and the community of believers.

During his formative years, Pastor Lane's family relocated to San Francisco, where he completed his primary and secondary education. In 1984, while in college, he experienced a life-altering encounter with Christ and embraced Him as his savior. Being part of a lineage of ministers, he recognized God's unmistakable calling on his life, delivering his inaugural sermon on January 27, 1985.

In 1987, he obtained a dual Business Administration and Economics degree from Saint Mary's College of California.

Since 1998, Pastor Lane has faithfully shepherded Neighborhood Baptist Church as its pastor. Possessing excellent teaching and leadership gifts, he leaves an indelible impact on the lives of countless individuals. His overarching vision revolves around equipping and empowering believers to embrace the abundant blessings that God has in store for them.

In addition to his pastoral duties, Pastor Lane assumed the positions of Athletic Director and Head Football Coach at St. Patrick-St. Vincent Catholic High School in Vallejo, CA, in 2014. As a coach, he successfully led his teams to several championships, including a State Championship in 2016.

Thrive: Igniting Your Fire for a Fulfilled Life

Known to his students as "Coach Hawk," he's made significant contributions to the lives of young student-athletes through these roles.